FINANCIAL ADVISORS
in **Banks** and
Credit Unions

Your **BLUEPRINT** for **SUCCESS**

ALEX SPENCER, CRPC,® CSSCS®

Financial Advisors in Banks and Credit Unions: Your Blueprint for Success

by Alex Spencer, CRPC®, CSSCS®

Published by Spencer Consulting Team, LLC
Copy editing and proofreading: Steph Spector
Book design and composition: Kim Scott/Bumpy Design
Cover and interior illustrations (pages 7, 81, and 137): Zenzen/Shutterstock.com

ISBN: 978-1-7377511-0-6

For consulting, speaking information, bulk orders, and more resources, please visit www.bankadvisorblueprint.com.

For Annie, Olivia, Sophia, Lulu, Croix, and Leo

CONTENTS

FOREWORD

by Don Connelly

When you find a book that tells you in detail how to get better at your job, read it!

Alex Spencer lives in the wisdom space. He has spent more than twenty years in the bank and credit union channel. That means that for more than twenty years, he has observed the habits of the greatest producers in this industry. A lot of authors *tell* you what to do. Alex shows you *how* to do it.

This book focuses on the three fundamental things every advisor needs to know: how to get more appointments, how to motivate people to take your advice, and how to grow your business. One of the great conundrums in a financial advisor's world is that running the business gets in the way of growing the business. Alex explains how to solve that riddle.

Don't read this book and put it on a shelf. Keep it in or on your desk. Write in it and refer to it. *Financial Advisors in Banks and Credit Unions: Your Blueprint for Success* is not just another book. It is a manual for financial institution advisors who want to progress to the next level.

Every advisor interviewed for this manual does more than $1,000,000 gross revenue per year. You no longer have to figure it out for yourself. You can find out, here, how the great ones do it.

To paraphrase a famous proverb:

To know the road ahead, ask those looking back.

INTRODUCTION

After selling life insurance in college, I did a brief stint at a national investment firm. Soon I found myself looking for a better way to do business, so I joined a bank.

Success came quickly to me, and even better, I discovered that I really enjoyed working with clients, making practical use of the knowledge I had amassed in my training. I adapted to the bank environment, and four years in, I was offered a sales management position. Without putting much thought into it, I took the leap, walked away from my book of business, and took on the new challenge. It didn't take long to learn that it was the right decision: my passion was helping advisors grow their businesses. Helping people fulfilled me.

After several years, I figured out that I could have a greater impact on more people's lives through wholesaling. I could make money based on my passion for helping others—and I never had to worry about who called in sick or who accidentally dropped their computer in the pool. I met more advisors, learned how they ran their businesses, and had even more advisors to share my ideas with. I spent almost ten years doing that—wholesaling, specifically to advisors in banks and credit unions—before getting recruited to serve as the national sales manager of a broker-dealer that competed in the bank and credit union market.

Among other things, my responsibilities were to sell investment programs to bank and credit union CEOs and to recruit, hire, train, and manage financial advisors. While this offered me yet another way to expand my experience and skill set, I realized that it was a deviation from helping advisors grow their businesses. I was spending more time with human resources, the legal department, and accounting than actually talking about what I love.

Which is when I learned that *your* business—not *the* business—was my passion. So I found my way back to wholesaling exclusively to bank and credit union advisors, where I could once again impact financial advisors' businesses and see results. Advisors who I work with know that I am a student of the business—I'm constantly studying their approach and exchanging ideas with them about practice management and soft-selling skills.

I tell you this because it is important context for this book: I have met hundreds and hundreds of advisors who are *all in banks and credit unions*, and I have seen everyone's seat from many different perspectives. For years I have helped them grow their books of business, their earnings, and their teams. I have hired, trained, coached, motivated, and even sold to them. Perhaps most importantly, I have sat in the seat and been an advisor myself.

Many advisors, no matter the environment they're in, face the same challenges. And don't take that as just my opinion; I've spent more than twenty years observing what the great advisors do well and what the underperforming ones do poorly.

In preparation for this book, I also conducted a series of

interviews. While really good advisors exist at all levels of production, I made the decision to interview only those who were producing gross revenue greater than $1,000,000 per year. I haven't written about every possible idea that could improve your business, but you can rest assured that the majority of the ideas in this book come from advisors who have used these strategies to get (and stay) where most people want to be.

There are numerous books about sales, some specifically directed at financial advisors. There is, however, very little content available that's specifically geared toward advisors in banks and credit unions. I suggest you still read those other books, as it is beyond the scope of this book to train you on how to be, generally speaking, a financial advisor. My goal is to train you on the nuances of delivering financial advice in a bank or credit union and to give you a blueprint for running your business, one that has proven successful in the past.

I have seen many good advisors spend several successful years in a wirehouse, as an insurance agent or independent advisor—who had been hired into the bank setting and failed.

Why did they fail? Because they didn't understand these three objectives:

- How to prospect and get more appointments

- How to sell in the way that the prospect or client wants to buy

- How to run a business efficiently so it scales activity and results

This book will cover these topics in three parts, each part broken down into chapters. Treat these parts as a playbook—and know that you can't run all the plays at the same time. Hopefully, you'll see how the plays fit together, and you'll learn when to focus on each play respectively and when it's appropriate to adopt certain strategies into your business plan.

Part One is about creating and maintaining a pipeline of prospects and clients. Above all, whether you are new to the business, new to the banking or credit union environment, or just want to raise your game after years of average performance, remember: don't try to do it all at once. That will overwhelm and discourage you. As I will suggest later in the book, be purposeful, controlled, and strategic when planning your business.

Part Two outlines a strategy for making sales. You will learn how to identify when to take someone straight down the full financial planning sales path and when to solve a problem and build a relationship over time. This part will cover selling to prospects in a way that appeals to them. People do not like to be sold to, but they do love to *buy*. Get out of the way and let the sale happen.

Part Three is what makes it all manageable and repeatable. It's about how to build the "business" part of your business: a controlled plan for assembling your team, promoting your business, and organizing your day.

I want to address something else that may have already crossed your mind. I am acutely aware of the differences between banks and credit unions. I have worked with many advisors—as well as senior executives and CEOs—in both banks and credit unions. And believe me, I understand the differences and the contention between the two. The reality is, no matter which business model an advisor is in, they'll face similar challenges. This said, I've reserved the last chapter specifically for credit union advisors, addressing the differences in culture and how to leverage those differences in the credit union space. For brevity's sake, throughout the book, I will be referring to both business models as "banks." No offense intended.

As you read this book, I invite you to remember the real business we are in: *the people business.*

Without people, we have nothing to do. No one to talk to. We cannot develop a book of business unless we have a way to reach lots and lots of people. To retain clients and develop long-term relationships with them, we need to know how to connect with them deeply and sincerely. We need to know what it means to treat people right.

Success happens when you develop connections to people, build others' trust in you, and practice ethically and consistently. You can only run a "people business" if you really, truly like people and allow them to like you, too. I mention this because one trait that top producers share is they genuinely like people. They don't just tolerate others, as many do. They care about who they're working with and enjoy their company. Whether it's clients, bank staff, their sales managers, wholesalers, their back office, or the cleaning crew, top producers just treat people as they want to be treated.

Before we get started, let me share one more story. Once, at a conference, I was helping host an advisor best practices panel. One of the top producers onstage was a quiet type from the deep South. He was known for not saying much but also for being incredibly successful. He managed almost as much in assets as his credit union had in assets.

Advisors fired questions around prospecting, planning, and product at the trio of producers. Then, suddenly, this advisor spoke up.

In his deep southern accent, he said, "Now y'all know, none of this matters if you aren't working at least forty hours a week."

The room went very quiet. You could hear the proverbial pin drop . . . on a carpet. *Really* quiet.

In other words, I know many of us got into the business because of the autonomy it provides. But don't confuse that as permission to not put the hours in and not do the work. If this is a lifestyle job for you, and you're not concerned with growing your income, that's your choice. And in that case, please keep on reading. I believe some of these strategies will make your job easier and give you more time to accomplish your life-styling.

But if you picked up this book because you want to join the elite in this business, you simply can't execute these strategies and see enough people in thirty hours per week to make a go of it. It won't happen for you.

For what it's worth, for this book I interviewed the largest producer I personally know—a gentleman grossing well over $3 million per year. I told him to call me anytime for the interview.

He called me just a few minutes after 6 a.m.

He was in his office.

Part One

BUILDING YOUR BUSINESS

It was 2000. I was a twenty-five-year-old financial advisor, already tired of knocking on doors. The tech bubble was bursting, and I was in Austin, Texas, where people were really feeling the infamous dot-com crash. Knocking on doors was less fun when everyone was losing money compared to when everyone was picking stocks and riding high.

I interviewed with a regional bank. The hiring manager suggested I go meet with one of their successful brokers who could vouch for his suggestion that the bank environment was not only good for practicing my profession, but would be easier than being independent. I made the drive to Bee Cave, Texas, into suburbs that had been fueled largely by the tech bubble. I met with a nice, young, intelligent advisor who said words that would stick with me to this day: "The bank breeds laziness."

He wasn't talking about bank staff or bankers or bank managers. He wasn't talking about that particular branch, or that particular regional bank. He was talking about all banks. And he was talking about advisors.

He explained to me that it's easy to feel busy in a bank. Every few minutes, people are walking in the door. At any time of the day, someone's in the breakroom. There always seems to be some service work to do. That, he said, is what made it easy to feel like you were gaining real momentum in your business, while in fact, you weren't.

It was good food for thought. His words really had me looking over my own shoulder, so to speak, to make sure I wasn't just acting busy but genuinely executing tactics that built my book of business.

When I was with a brokerage firm, my first decision every day was to decide what time I was going to start knocking on doors. But in banks, I see so many advisors who don't consistently engage in prospecting activities.

After I decided to join a bank, I could see what the fellow meant: it was very easy to fall into that trap of pretend-productivity. At a bank, your first thought should still be, *What am I going to do today to get in front of someone new?* You don't have to perform every marketing activity ever invented. But you have to do *something* concrete on a daily basis—you need to use one or more tactics that someone successful has been doing to build his or her own book of clients, and use them in a consistent manner.

Even the most successful book brokers who are no longer covering branches are looking to grow their business. They—we— all want more prospects. Without prospects, you have no one to turn into a new client.

Be systematic, try tactics over several months (once won't usually be enough), track effectiveness, and if the tactic gets you the results you are looking for, keep doing it.

In these pages, I'll give you many "things to try." When one of the tactics works the first, second, or third time for you, ramp it up. Stick with it. Fine-tune it. Certainly do more of it. But keep learning and perfecting it by asking others in our business how they are doing the same thing.

Don't assume there is something better out there, only to try each tactic just one time. Again, once won't pull it off! Be persistent. When you get a higher return on efforts, figure out what you did differently that got you there. Take notes. Keep your numbers. Refer to them. Brainstorm ways to improve even more.

Even as you see your business grow, don't stop.

The way I see it, one of two things might happen when you pump the brakes after experiencing growth:

One, you might feel busy because you've made a whole lot of appointments. So you slack off on prospecting, and ... your pipeline dries up entirely. Prospect with tactics in this book every day!

Two, you might encounter a "plateau." Using prospecting tactics, you've gotten up into the $200,000 to $500,000 range of gross revenue, and now you feel proud. Yes, you are making a decent living, maybe more than you've made in your career. I appreciate that it's time for a pat on the back. But having gained enough new clients to feel successful and busy, you stop executing the same effective prospecting tactics—and you don't even attempt to add new approaches. You cannot make significant leaps in your business to eventually go beyond $500,000 and get to $750,000 or the million-plus mark ... the next year. Yet it *is* possible to make that jump in one year when your machine is tested, well-oiled, and efficient. But as professional athletes will tell you, even in the off-season, there are no days off from training. (Or, in our case, prospecting.) Those athletes earn the big bucks for *training, working out, and sweating*. They play the big games for free. And that's pretty much how it is when you are a financial advisor building a clientele inside a bank or credit union.

In this first group of chapters that I call "Building Your Business," we will look at some ways to get in front of more people. It's on you to decide which of these tactics is best for you. Just know this: even if you do everything else poorly, by seeing more people, you will close more business.

CHAPTER 1

MAKING CALLS

No one *loves* making calls. Most don't even like it. Some will tolerate it in tiny doses. Others just can't pick up the phone no matter how beneficial the outcome might be.

Using the phone, getting on the horn, giving someone a buzz, smiling and dialing—whatever name you use for this activity, it's unavoidable. Calling is at the heart of connecting with new prospects, building a pipeline of prospects who become clients, and staying in touch with current clients to provide them more services down the road. You have to do it!

If you're coming from another investment firm and transitioning into a bank environment, you will start to feel very busy. When that feeling sets in, picking up the phone may be one of the first activities you cut back on. And though that's so easy to justify, it's a mistake. At the bank, the phone is still your best ally. No matter your current production level, if you want to increase your bottom line, it's no secret: start making more phone calls.

Rest assured, though. Making calls from the bank is not like making cold calls. (It's definitely not the smile-and-dial of the old days when you were dialing people who didn't know you, and—a lot of the time—weren't even familiar with your company. That's a true telemarketing cold call.) The very nice thing about calling from the bank is that almost all the calls, if not 100% of them, are warm calls to some degree. The people at the other end of the line may be strangers to you, but they're the bank's customers. Introduce yourself using the bank's name, and the recipient will perk up with recognition. That's not a cold call. They know the brand. And that makes them open to listening to you. Not a cold call at all!

Here's what the goal is *not*. It's not to make the sale on that call, profile, or talk product. The goal is usually to *get an appointment*. The silver lining is it's much easier to get appointments at the bank than anywhere else. Because most people go to the bank with some regularity, they don't view it as an ordeal.

Selling doesn't have to be a face-to-face business, but it's much easier when it is. So try not to spend a lot of time selling over the phone. If the client is in another state, or for whatever reason they can't come to you, and there's no way you're going to get in front of them, then, yes, sell them over the phone. No harm doing it, and it has certainly been done many times before. But don't make the phone your primary means of making sales; you want to get in front of the prospect or client and have an opportunity to build a relationship, increase your closing ratio, and gather more assets.

Call With an Action Item

Have a clear and justified reason to be calling.

There are many "easy" reasons: you met somebody in the lobby, they attended one of your educational workshops, you get lists from the bank, or you're calling based on CD maturities or high-balance money markets. Any of those examples—or similar ones—are clear, justified reasons for picking up the phone. If a CD is coming due, a decision has to be made about it. Maybe the decision will be to do nothing and let the CD roll. But money-in-motion is a great reason to call.

Not only is a money-in-motion call more actionable, but it also gives you more credibility. Why? Because if you possess such information about the person you're calling, you must be connected to their bank. Banks will provide different levels of information to you to use for these calls. Keep in mind that any information you have ties you in with the bank because it creates the impression in the person's mind over the phone that you're part of the bank from a trust, security, and convenience standpoint. That's exactly what you want.

I mention this tip about client information that bank management gives you because I have spoken to many advisors who say their calls bear no fruit. When I ask them what their goal is when calling clients, they say, "Just to let our clients know that I can be their financial advisor." Those aren't necessarily bad calls to make, don't get me wrong. Your appointment ratio and close ratio, however, go up with money-in-motion calls.

Scripting. Even if you get minimal information about the client or account, these are still great calls to make; don't let that be an excuse for not calling.

You need to check with your compliance department and make sure you know exactly what needs to be disclosed, but the more of an impression you can make on the prospect that you're calling from their bank (even if just physically), the greater trust and recognition you build with that prospect.

Borrow the trust that they have with the bank. The more verbiage you include, the more you muddy the water. In identifying yourself, include what you have to include, but nothing more. State just enough information for the client on the end of the line to start nodding in recognition, feeling that he "knows you" and that "oh, yes, I think I do have money due around now ... "

There are a few types of prospecting calls you can make, including referrals that you receive from the branch, calls off of a list that you're given by the bank, and scheduled follow-ups promised to a prospect. My suggestion would be to create a script for each type.

And by the way, never, ever call a client and say, "Hi, this is John from your bank." Be professional! *Everyone* knows at least five guys named John. Which John are you? *Many* people have more than one bank. Which bank are you from?

I'm going to focus first on those warm prospecting calls.

Here's the ideal script for a call about a CD coming due, not including what you'd need to say to meet compliance requirements:

"Hello, John Brown! This is Jane Blue from XYZ Bank—your bank on Main Street. I see you have a CD coming due. I'd like to set up a time for us to get together and decide what to do next with it."

And here's the ideal script for a call about a high-dollar money market or savings account:

"Hello, John Brown! This is Jane Blue from XYZ Bank—your bank on Main Street. I see you have an unusually high balance stacking up in your savings account. I'd like to set up a time for us to get together and decide what to do next with it, so you do better with the earnings."

These aren't quite as powerful as CD maturities, as there is no required decision to be made but to create a sense of urgency with your voice. If needed, throw in an additional clincher question: "Have you thought about doing something better?" It's that simple.

Again, check with compliance to see what you need to share with prospects. As a rule of thumb, the less information you can give them over the phone, the better. You haven't discussed anything you are going to talk to them about. You just want to set up a time to meet. Telling them the specific branch location where you expect to meet is helpful, especially if there are fifteen branches all over town and you're at the branch on Main Street.

I repeat: the less information you give them, the better. And I don't mean that to sound deceitful in any way. We're not trying to trick them, but the challenge is there are certain phrases that cause what I call "the client's wall" to go up. You also don't want to get roped into a sales presentation over the phone.

There are sales books that talk about power words or good words to use versus bad words to use in terms of positioning yourself in sales. It's remedial sales training, but it's super important. And there's a whole different set of words you have to be cognizant of and avoid when calling bank clients. "Financial advisor" is not a scary word in many scenarios. But if you're calling a list of clients from a bank, for example, and you say, "I'm the financial advisor," that's intimidating. That's a word that might put the client's wall up, with this unvoiced question: *Oh, what does he want to sell me?*

Clients may be looking for *help*, but they aren't looking for a financial advisor. The words "financial advisor" comes with a number of connotations or misnomers that may not be good for you. It will take the call down a road you don't want to take.

A few other words to avoid: *meeting* (use *visit*, as meeting sounds very formal), *investment, financial planner, annuity, risk, long-term, change, cost,* and *fees.* Those are all words that can put a prospect on their heels.

That said, from a compliance standpoint, if you're going to present the product over the phone—the prospect is out of state or can't come into the office—don't worry about the fact that *annuity* is a bad word. If you're presenting an annuity, you have to tell the client it's an annuity. My word-choice advice is primarily for prospecting calls and trying to set appointments.

Make an Appointment, Not a Sale

Many times, clients will follow up with a question. You ask for an appointment time, or if they've considered doing something better, and they respond with, "What's your best rate?" or "Are you going to talk to me about annuities?" or "Is it FDIC insured?"

And again, I would be very careful of how far you take that conversation. It might take you down the road of presenting a product, which leads to making a sale over the phone. You do not want this call to be a great opportunity for the prospect to gather information.

Advantageous to you in avoiding sale-talk: people are anxious to get off the phone. They don't want to be sold anything. Especially the first time a client hears from you, they may feel some pressure during your call.

If they are not receptive to your invitation, turn the tables when you can. Here's how. You can be "anxious" to get *them* off the phone, as a courtesy:

"It sounds like you're busy with the holidays. Why don't I call you back in January and we can talk some more?"

(Doesn't have to be holiday season. Replace with whatever makes sense.)

Let's say you call them back in January. You now have the opportunity to say, "You asked me to call you."

Now, you're doing something for them since *they* asked *you* for the callback. Nine times out of ten, the client will agree that you should call them back at some point, just to get off the phone. Or they'll just make that appointment with you—in January, or next week—and that is exactly your goal.

Another way of turning the tables is to pivot as soon as the client asks a question. Make your goal not to answer their question on the phone but to land an appointment at the bank.

Say, "It sounds like you've got some questions. Why don't we plan on getting together? Is Thursday afternoon good for you to come into the bank, or is Friday morning better?"

This is a strategic time to suggest an appointment because now you are doing something for them. They have questions, and you are suggesting two alternative times for a visit so that they may have their questions answered. Why two times? That makes it clear, at least subliminally, that an appointment is not an option. It will take place! But the time of the appointment is the client's choice.

Turn List Calls Into Relationship Calls

Your bank may be progressive and have a contact management system or customer relationship management software (CRM). But most banks and credit unions do not yet have the sales culture to require these tools across the company. Commercial lenders and mortgage lenders have more of a sales culture, so they're used to it. But the frontline bank staff is usually not opening a CD for somebody and then putting it into a contact management database.

After entering the bank branch environment, you may have

realized that nobody else was keeping track of their conversations. That may have even led you to think, *Maybe I don't need to keep track of conversations, either.*

But tracking contacts and setting follow-ups is something you should do. *Consistently.* You need to because you are running a business for the long term . . . and nobody's memory is that sharp!

I have found that a lot of bank advisors do use a CRM to keep track of current clients, but not prospects. Again, you are running a business for the long term, so use it for both groups of people. The names you collect now may come from lists, educational workshops, referrals, or community events that the bank sponsors, and that will be your prospect pool of people to solicit. I call that initial call or contact a *list call.* You are calling them off a list. You don't know them or their needs yet. Their name is simply on a potential list or prospect list for your business.

My goal for you is to turn those list calls into what I call *relationship calls.* A relationship call means you have already spoken to the client before, you know some of their needs, you have some reason to call them back, and they are somewhere in your sales funnel. There is some sort of engagement or connection there. And while the next call may be scheduled for six months or a year out, the sales process has begun. You aren't simply firing through a list. (Think you can remember details six months or a year out? *Yeah.* Use that software to track all your contacts.)

Let's say you're calling off a CD maturity list. You use your script for those calls, encouraging folks to come in and see you to talk about what to do with the CD.

One customer cuts you off, responding, "I just want to leave it in a one-year CD. Let's just let it roll."

Okay, now it feels like the conversation might be over, like you don't have much room to convince that person to see you in the office.

Your new goal is to give yourself a reason to call them back.

"Okay, Mr. Smith," you might say. "Sounds like you just want to leave the money in a CD. Let's do that. We have a special one-year rate." (Remember that all rates are *special*.) "Why don't I call you back in one year, and then we'll get together, sit down, and figure out what to do with it?"

Another reason to set up a future call? You see that they have other bank accounts.

"I see you have another CD coming due next month. Why don't I call you back next month on that one?"

Whatever it is, always find a reason to call that client back! Enter them in your contact management software and set yourself a reminder to get them on the phone. Then do so, as promised.

Like any other salesperson would do, focus on picking up on personal cues from the client, and you'll find a reason to call them back. Did they mention they're going on vacation? Has their ten-year-old been gifted a new puppy for her birthday last week? Is their oldest off to college in September? Use these conversational tidbits. They're grist for the call-back, relationship-building mill. Put the information in your notes and bring that tidbit of personal news up in future calls. "I remember you said you were sending your child off to college last month . . . " and build this relationship based on the conversation about it.

This is what's key: put this information into a contact management system (Salesforce, Redtail, or whatever platform or software you use) to track these conversations and to jog your memory at follow-up time.

I know I sound like a sales manager here, but trust me. It

works. Because with this information, the first time you call them, you'll have some chance of moving the sales process along with them. Let's say you have a 20% chance of selling them or maybe getting an appointment. The second time you call, that percentage goes up. Maybe in 50% of your second calls, you'll be able to get an appointment. The third time you call them, that number will go up even more—say, to 60% or 70%. And from my experience in the bank environment, by the fifth call, they will be able to recognize your name and say something personal to you, such as, "Oh, hi, how have you been, Alex?" Or they'll be impressed by your "memory." ("Oh, Alex, I'm touched that you remembered my oldest went off to college last September.")

Clients will come to understand that when you call them, it's to try to help them. They just have to do their part to build the relationship. After getting on that many calls with you, and seeing how you remember the personal information they share, they'll be impressed by your service!

If you are still not convinced about using a software tracking system, ponder this: America is so used to bad service that if you tell someone you'll call them in three months and actually do it, you're going to surprise them. If you do it again—promise to call and follow through—whether it's a month, three months, or a year later, they'll be blown away by your service and (truth be told) by the attention you are paying *to them*. Everyone loves attention! Everyone likes to think others remember the stories they tell.

In the bank environment, if you've called a bank customer five times over a year, two years, three years, you're going to get a meeting with them. You can parlay that new relationship development into an invitation like, "Well, next time you're in the branch, ask for me and let's at least shake hands. It'll be a pleasure to meet you face-to-face!" But then keep calling them.

Keep those names and the information attached to them. Turning those *list calls* into *relationship calls* is important because at some point maybe you don't get a list. Or maybe you get a bad list. You've always got to have a group of people you can go back and market to. The first year that you're in a bank, many of your calls will be list calls. Certainly in the first three to six months—they'll *all* be list calls. But every time you get another relationship call that pops up on your to-do list, that's going to be an easier prospect, an easier conversation with more information to build on. And two years, three years, four years in, you won't need as many list calls because you'll have hundreds and hundreds of *relationship calls* that are well in progress and turning into new business.

Know the Bank's Products

It is good to always have bank products in your back pocket while making these calls. You want to connect yourself with the bank in the prospect's mind. That you're the guy or the gal *in the bank* is part of your brand. So if they ask a question about a product, you should be well-educated on the bank's products and able to answer unswervingly, without missing a beat.

Yes, I know you don't make any money on bank products. Sometimes those products are even your competition. But that's part of being in a bank.

If you call someone from a CD list, know the CD rates. When they say, "Oh, by the way, what's a one-year CD paying right now?" you'll damage your credibility as their resource at the bank if you don't answer immediately and without hesitation. This is

Call Preparation 101. I recommend always knowing a short-term CD rate (or whatever product information you need), so that you have a reason to call back or meet again sooner than later.

On Leaving Voicemails

Voicemails are inevitable. Everyone screens calls. Even when someone they like is calling, someone might not answer the phone. Not everyone will call you back, but it should be a pretty good ratio.

Voicemail is definitely not a valid excuse to not make phone calls. But we have to be smart about the voicemails that we leave. And again, I've got to give the compliance disclosure. You need to check with your bank or broker-dealer to see what is absolutely necessary in terms of the information you provide. But here's the ideal script:

"Hello, this is a message for John Brown. Mr. Brown, this is Mary Blue from XYZ Bank, your bank on Main Street. Please give me a call back when you have the opportunity. I'm at the bank, and here is my direct line: 222-222-2222."

Again, the less information, the better.

It's common sense. If you leave the person very little information and say, "I'm from your bank," they should feel a reason to call you back.

Our goal is to create a sense of urgency, but not worry. And there's nothing wrong with that. That's not something we should apologize for. A client's interest rate, liquidity, and financial goals should be fairly urgent and important to that client. We're trying to help them with their situation.

Keep at it on the phone. I know calling isn't the fun part of the business. Airline pilots do the tedious, repetitive, routine, and procedural "grunt work" before each flight, and they don't like it any more than you like picking up the phone. The pilots do it, though, because it's a critical part of their process. Making those warm calls will work for you, too, and that's a fact. When you use this strategy, your calls will get easier every day, and you will have results to show for it.

CHAPTER 2

EDUCATIONAL WORKSHOPS

Y ou no longer put on "seminars." You put on educational workshops, which aren't the old-school, played out, over-used, salesy seminars you might be thinking of—they're a means for marketing your business and generating leads. In a workshop, you aren't pushing product; you are a subject-matter expert presenting useful information and facilitating informed decisions.

The Goals of an Educational Workshop

When they are done correctly, some advisors can build their business using educational workshops as their primary means of marketing. I've seen it happen!

So, why might you do an educational workshop?

- **To meet people.** Get new names to add to the top of your funnel.

- **To get appointments.** When a workshop is well-executed, you can expect at *least* half of the attendees to request an appointment with you. Depending on the topic, those appointments may or may not lead to quick sales. In all cases, they allow you to build a relationship that will lead to more sales and more referrals.

- **To raise program awareness.** People can't buy what they are not aware of. When you look at the statistics industry-wide for the number of bank customers who are even aware that the bank has an investment program and a licensed financial advisor, the numbers are incredibly low. (In some markets, they're even in the single digits.)

- **To promote your brand inside the bank as an educator.** You are bringing value to the financial lives of clients. It is good for them to see another side of you that's about educating clients, making sure they're doing the right things with their money. Also, bank management will—if they are smart, and they usually are—see the added value you bring to the bank through that educational effort.

Getting Started

One good way to get started is to incorporate your educational workshop topic into any kind of educational series that the bank offers. Like educational workshops on buying your first house, or how to apply for a mortgage. You can approach the marketing department to ask if you can tie your workshop in with anything that the bank is doing or going to do in the near future as part of their education series. They may even market your workshop alongside those other events.

Don't expect your first educational workshop to produce a phenomenal result in terms of attendance. It's like launching a new retail business. You have to get the word out first. But the more your client base or the bank's client base sees your invitation becoming more of a regular thing, the more they realize, "Oh, okay, this is real. This is not a one-time deal. These look like things I want to learn about."

I once worked with an advisor who was very consistent with his approach. He did one educational workshop per quarter. In the first year, he had six or eight people show up for every workshop. Now, keep in mind that this creates twenty to thirty new leads for him that year. That's a start. But with his consistency, every year, the attendance increased slightly. And after five or six years of doing it, he was filling the room with thirty to fifty people regularly, four times per year.

Welcome that kind of momentum by being consistent. First, you'll attract people who attend one of your events, then see your next topic come up, and then attend that workshop . . . and then another one. Soon, you've got a relationship with that person. Maybe they bring someone new along with them the next time. Every time you get in front of these people, your chance of them becoming a client increases. They see value in the information. They trust your knowledge base. They may even like you! You may even have some downtime for some conversation with them before and after your workshop.

How to Send Invitations

Invite people as inexpensively as you can. You may need to partner with the bank's marketing department. They may do email marketing with their bank list for you or send snail mail in bulk. They might be able to design educational workshop materials for you. Even if the bank does not provide you a list of people to call, you may be able to approach management and persuade them to promote client education within the bank. They may be much more helpful about giving you people to do mailings or email blasts.

Another kind of guerilla-style marketing is to layer your promotion:

- Put it on the bank or credit union's website.

- Hang up signage in the bank lobby.

- Print flyers and give them to the bank staff to hand out at the door as clients enter.

- Train the bank staff on the event so that they can talk about it while handing out flyers to individuals.

Those are all good ways to pick up additional attendance while the primary methods of email and snail mail invitations build the primary response.

Send Lots of Invitations

It can take several thousand email invitations to fill a room. Expect very, very low percentage turnouts. Don't take that personally. Marketing professionals will state that 2%-3% returns are typical—and depending on the product, even outstanding! So don't send out a hundred invitations or emails and expect a crowd. This is why I think email is great. It's inexpensive, and you reach thousands with one click of a key on your keyboard.

Ask your assistant to make follow-up calls to remind people. Even people who want to attend an event sometimes just forget. A reminder will get an extra number of people through the door.

Asking for RSVPs

It might be you ask them to call or email to register ("It's free, but only to registered attendees"), with the logistical advantage to you of knowing in advance:

- How many are attending. If the number is too small, you know who to cancel. In this case, simply call the prospect and ask them to come in for an appointment. If the number is too large for the pre-planned meeting space, you have time to get a larger room.

- How many chairs to reserve and set up.

- If you have handouts, how many to print.

I worked with one advisor who would market seminars but never had the intent of holding the workshop. He would call anyone that RSVP'd a few days before the workshop and give an excuse why it had to be canceled, but then set an appointment to discuss how the topic affects their financial plan. He simply cuts out the middleman and sells it as a benefit to just address their needs and concerns. I'm not saying it's the right thing to do or the honest thing to do, but it can work (but only from time to time).

Picking a Day, Time, and Length for a Workshop

Thursday is the best day for an educational workshop, followed by Tuesday, Wednesday, and then Monday—in that order. If you're in an area where Wednesday is a very popular day for people to go to church, then don't schedule on a Wednesday. That's a local community awareness you need to develop. I have seen a few advisors have success with Saturday afternoons if they are targeting retirees because every day is Saturday to them. But be aware of complicated logistics if the bank isn't normally open on Saturday.

As far as timing goes, keep in mind the market you're soliciting. Retirees might welcome a breakfast or luncheon workshop. If you are inviting individuals who still work, a short-and-sweet luncheon workshop is also good for a "two birds, one stone" (eat-and-learn during free time) approach. But generally, if people you want to talk to are still working, keep your educational workshops to the evening.

When you set an evening start time, consider participant travel times and traffic. Generally, if everyone gets off work at about 5 p.m., maybe you want to start your workshop at around 6 p.m. And if you're in a really small town, maybe even 5:30 p.m. The problem is if people have too much time, and if you pick a 6:30 p.m. or 7 p.m. start time, they're going to go home first because they've got too much downtime. If they go home, they get comfortable and then don't want to go back out. So the strategy is to give them enough time to get there without being too rushed, but not enough time to go home.

You don't want the educational workshop to last much longer than an hour. Reserve time for an introduction and housekeeping items (5 minutes), the body of the presentation (30–45 minutes), and a Q&A period and evaluations (10–15 minutes).

The Ideal Location

I'm not a fan of the steak dinner educational workshops. Those feel like seminars. And I'm not a proponent of doing educational workshops in restaurants at all. Some restaurants have private rooms that you can block off, and some don't. But even if they do, the rooms tend to be noisy with a lot of distractions. You're just not going to present yourself in a way that's educational and professional in such an environment. Save restaurants for client appreciation events.

The best places for hosting educational workshops are at the bank. People appreciate a casual atmosphere in a professional space. Consider a conference room, training room, or board room—or even hold them in the lobby after the lobby closes. Obviously, you need permission from the bank to do this, but after the lobby closes, gather all the chairs and move them into a seating area. Set up a portable screen and a table for the projector. Arrange the room so everybody will be able to see the screen. I've seen these educational workshops being phenomenally successful. The environment puts people at ease and makes it easier for them to learn and participate.

Hosting a workshop at the bank is great because it's free of cost to you and the participants, and it ties your brand to the bank. Plus, it's just easy. You don't have to go about making any formal reservations, putting down deposits, or ensuring a minimum number of attendees. It makes it an easy, repeatable process.

A few other low-pressure environments work, too. Some towns have community centers, senior centers, community college spaces, or public library meeting rooms that you might be able to reserve for little or nothing. Plus, those spaces tend to be quiet, making it easy to hear every voice in the room. I think that helps create an educational environment.

Food

Sometimes, you have to figure out how to feed your attendees. Certainly if you're hosting a lunchtime educational workshop, or if people are expected to come on their lunch break, you have to offer food—if only a brown bag lunch or a make-your-own-sandwich buffet—because that may be their only time to eat. If you have a smaller group, you could take orders and do sandwich boxes. Subway is inexpensive and does the trick. You aren't trying to buy business.

For evening educational workshops, you have a couple of different food options. The key is you want them to be comfortable. You want them to like you. You want them to appreciate the event. But it should not come across as though you're *buying them* in order to get their business. By far the most popular option I've seen for evening educational workshops is some kind of snack (either an after-dinner or pre-dinner snack) and coffee and water. When your information and presentation have been both useful and entertaining, the attendees really don't care about the food.

Attendee Evaluations

Getting feedback from the people in attendance is probably the most important part of your workshop.

Early on in my workshops, I'll say something like this: "As you know, nothing is free, and this educational workshop is not free either. Your fee for attending this workshop is this evaluation that you complete for me." And then I'll hold one up. "Your fee, the cost to attend this, is filling this out. And I'm going to ask a personal favor from you, to take two minutes when we're done, to let us know how we did. I'm a big boy—I can take criticism—so be honest. We want to make this better for groups in the future." I use the words "personal favor" specifically because people recognize a favor as something that they can do for you. When you've shown them value for the past hour, and they've learned something that was really new and useful, they won't mind evaluating your efforts.

At the end of the workshop, I will again say, "Remember that personal favor I asked for? We're going to hand out this evaluation now, and I will ask again, please take just two minutes to let us know what you think."

You might also add, "At the conclusion, my service specialist will be in the back of the room with my calendar. We have set aside time over the next two weeks to meet with anyone who is interested in setting up a time to visit."

And on the evaluation, there should be several straightforward, quick-to-answer, no-pressure questions:

- Were the contents of the workshop presented in a clear and understandable way?

- Will you be able to use the information in your personal financial decision-making?

- Was the location easy to access?

- Was the time and day of this event easy for you to schedule/attend?

- Suggestions to help improve our events?

- Which topics would you be interested in learning about in future events?

- Would you like to be contacted for a no-cost consultation to address how these topics affect your personal situation?

One of the main goals of an educational workshop, if you recall, is to get appointments. So that last question is a must. And when an educational workshop goes well, 50% of buying units should request an appointment. That's a good goal to strive for. (A "buying unit" may be an individual or a husband and wife/a couple, since the latter only counts for one appointment.) If they answer that final question with "yes," call them the next day. If they say no, send them a personal note to thank them for attending and invite them to contact you if you can be of service. If they do not answer that question, call them to invite them to meet with you.

Don't Delegate the Presenting

If you're the one who educates the attendees, there's a good chance that you're the one who will get their future business. Be the one at the front of the room unless you are not comfortable with public speaking. (And hey—if you are not at ease, get trained up! Join Toastmasters!) It is fine to use wholesalers, as they will often volunteer, but start practicing and keep practicing until you are comfortable being the presenter of your own workshop.

Your Presentation

Start with introductions. If a wholesaler or someone else is doing the speaking for the topic of the workshop, introduce yourself, your position in the bank, where your office is, how long you've been there, and what kind of people you work with. Then share a success story about the kinds of people you can help the most, like a retirement story.

Then have the main educational event. You may present the material yourself (again, this is best for building your business) or use another speaker.

Probably the most popular outside speaker is a product wholesaler. The benefit is that they generally have substantial public speaking experience. They do a lot of these educational workshops, and often the product vendor will have turnkey educational workshop content that you can use. Most wholesalers will make that part of their value to advisors' businesses.

Sometimes I've seen a sales manager who has a lot of public speaking experience come in and do some speaking.

Another option would be some kind of non-bank professional with the desired knowledge. If, for example, you're doing an educational workshop on estate planning, a local attorney can come in at no cost (since they're somewhat promoting themselves and their services). That's a great value-added approach that you can tie yourself into by talking about how it fits into your planning as a financial advisor.

Slideshow Coma

Presenters use PowerPoint slides on a screen to give people a visual of what they are saying, to put images to words. But be careful about putting people into what I call a PowerPoint coma. And if you show too many slides only with words or numbers on them (which is a risk in our business), then it defeats your purpose. Another move that can put people in a "coma" is when you read exactly what is on the slides and face the screen instead of the audience. Use graphs, tables, charts, or funny cartoon images. Minimal words. Face the audience and be the source of the words. Watch their reactions as you speak. Face them the whole time and *connect with them*—not your screen.

Be the Last Expert on Stage

Whoever presents for or with you, be the closer, and definitely be the leader of the question-and-answer session. You are the last person on stage, the one the audience remembers. The goal of this is to build business for you, the advisor, and it doesn't help anybody if people want to discuss their investment situation with a wholesaler, a sales manager, or someone else in the bank staff. *The goal is to give prominence to you as a financial advisor.* You are their future source of information, advice, options, and knowledge.

Leading the Q&A

Here is a quick tip for taking questions. In my experience, you will sometimes get questions that will clue you in on a very good prospect. Something like: "I am trying to decide if I should take my pension in payments or roll it over to an IRA, can I . . . ?"

When you hear that, an alarm in your head should be going off, alerting you that you need to meet this guy!

Respond with, "There could be a few moving parts to that question. Let's chat one-on-one for two minutes when we wrap up here, and let me then answer your question fully."

This will give you a chance to build a bit more rapport . . . and hopefully set an appointment!

Following Up After the Event

The key to achieving your goal of many leads and as many appointments after the workshop is follow up.

The first follow-up is for those who'd like a call from you. Now it is you who will make the commitment to them. "If you check 'Yes' on that last question, I will call you within the next 24 to 48 hours to set up a time to meet. If you check 'No,' that is okay. No one will call you—except to invite you to the next educational workshop I organize for you!" And include at the top of the form lined spaces for their name, address, email, and phone number so that you easily have contact information for the next day's call to them.

Educational Approach

The last thing I'll mention is the strategy for educating people. I tell advisors that we do these educational workshops to educate people, but make sure there's a strategy behind it. We want to educate people enough that they walk away having learned something, but we don't want to overeducate them.

With workshops on very complicated topics like Social Security or Medicare or annuities, attendees should feel like they learned something *but also realize it's too confusing to learn it all.* Perhaps they'll learn the general benefits of a subject, or maybe a well-selected detail or two—especially if you can dig up one juicy, valuable fact that few people actually know. But to personalize it to their case, make sure they still need you!

This strategy really gives you an opportunity to step up as the expert, and it gives you follow-up points and reasons they should come in and meet with you.

Remember, too, that your educational workshop should be fundamentally educational. It is definitely not a product pitch. Now, that's not to say that you absolutely cannot mention or explain products or differentiate products. But try to stay away from the "one-size-fits-all, here's an idea, here's what you need to do."

What, then, about specific product education? If there is a specific product that you find people do not understand, by all means, do an educational workshop on that *specific product.* But you have to keep it very neutral, and you have to be careful with this one. An example is annuities because annuities are largely misunderstood. You could do an educational workshop on what an annuity is or the different types of annuities that exist, but you want to keep it very general, high-level, and nonspecific in terms of what's the best or what people should do.

If it's a relevant topic that many people misunderstand, people will appreciate the education. But they still won't want a product pitch. Your educational goal should be, "Well, folks, now you know what annuities *really* are, and the next time you are thinking about which one might be most appropriate to your personal goals, you will know exactly what questions to ask me." Also, be very clear in the marketing of your educational workshops. Don't promote an educational workshop on annuities as a workshop on retirement income planning and then just talk about annuities being used for retirement income planning. Be clear that the advertised topic is what you will cover.

CHAPTER 3

BRANCH REFERRAL TRAINING

Referrals can and should be the lifeblood of your business. The best way to get referrals is to train people in the bank to send you prospects.

Your branch referral training has to be clear and specific so that branch employees feel comfortable sending you their best clients. After the training—whether it's informal or formal— the employees should be willing to allow you to help the bank's customers. Like any tactic or new strategy, personalize this time-tested framework so that it works for you.

Remember, just because you're at a bank doesn't mean you have a captive audience and don't have to prospect anymore. That's far from the truth. Prospecting, or finding new leads, is just as important when you're in a bank environment as when you're independent, but you go about it differently. There are a number of ways to prospect, but one of the most powerful means is to fully leverage the branch staff—and training them to send you referrals is that leverage.

Think about it. The bank's frontline staff see a new client every few minutes. This is a huge opportunity for them to refer to you. If only they knew how ...

Your Training Strategy

Training is not a once-and-done thing. You have to train and train and train and train. I've talked to advisors who say, "I do referral training every year at the beginning of the year." What? No! That's not nearly often enough. The first problem with that approach is that turnover for the average teller may be less than a year. When you do your referral training just once a year, half the staff's going to be gone and replaced before your next training rolls around. Some may never even see you at all.

So that's rule #1. You must do the referral training over and over and over, frequently, throughout the year. Literally every single chance you get to be in front of these people who will be your sources for referrals—you have to be training. Training is not an inoculation. It has to be repeated.

Short and Sweet Does It

Other services and business lines may be trying to get to the tellers and the bankers and the managers so that they'll promote their business line, which is what we should all be doing. So you have to make it clear and *very easily actionable.*

This is rule #2. Your training has to be short and to the point. Above all, it should give frontline bankers words they're comfortable saying to clients.

Find Out Where and When You Have Training Opportunities

What are the avenues for where you can deliver your referral training? Every bank I work with is different in terms of your opportunity and your "shelf space" (attention among all the business lines). Some banks are very accommodating to the advisor. In other banks, you literally get a once-a-year opportunity, and that's it.

Build relationships in your bank right from the start. Then you might be allowed to train every quarter. If you already get a training opportunity every quarter, then work with the branch managers to train every month. Ask for incremental gains as you develop internal relationships.

Training Groups

Ask to speak at branch manager meetings or any meeting of job families: tellers, personal bankers, or assistant managers. Attend branch huddles and do your two-minute training there. If the branch gets together once a week—some banks are very ambitious and hold a five-minute meeting every morning—ask for time once a week for the ninety-second training (especially if you see new faces, new tellers, or transferred-in staff at the meeting). Further, attend these meetings to be a part of the team, even if you don't have speaking time. When they know your face and your name, it *counts*.

Door Jamb Training

Training might take place in a formalized environment to many people at once, when you can arrange it. But don't discount the value of having little one-on-one conversations with some regularity and with everyone at the branch. In the course of any given day, all of us have such opportunities. They don't have to be scheduled. Sit down with people or lean on the door jamb and make sure they know you and what you offer your mutual clientele.

A warning, though: don't make your visits so long to where it is obvious you are talking about football or ice hockey. That doesn't sit well with management. They encourage training, but their employees have jobs to do.

And then, rule #3. Train informally even more often than formally. Seize every chance you can.

Trust Builds Your Business

The most important thing to know with referrals is that above everything else, the referrer has to like you and they have to trust you. They have to trust that you will not make them look bad for referring. The last thing you would want to do is sabotage their business or undermine a relationship.

That is why rule #4 is to be trustworthy; be likable. This is valid for any service business. One of the largest-producing bank advisors who I know personally *built his entire business through branch referrals*. I asked him how he did it, and he simply said, "I got them to like me."

Possibly the most trust you can build is opening an account for the bank employee. Many advisors have told me that their best referrals come from the staff member who has an account with them. Delaney Spencer is a teller; offer to open a CD and explain all about the benefits of CDs as you do it. Delaney will have seen the process, and you will have demystified what you do. Now? She refers clients to you. She might even add, "He'll explain everything to you and make it ever so easy!"

Other types of accounts you can open for bank staff: roll over old 401(k) plans for new employees; offer dollar-cost averaging accounts or term life insurance for younger employees. Again, explain in easy, repeatable terms what you are doing, so they turn around and tell clients, "He showed us how advantageous it was compared to what we'd been doing."

From a trust standpoint, if they give you money, then they should feel comfortable referring clients to you.

Longer Referral Training Sessions

Sometimes a longer training format may be available to you. Maybe you have thirty minutes, but you have to maintain a simple message for making referrals. Don't complicate it or confuse bank employees with too many details and unfamiliar terminologies. Instead, tell them about yourself. Tell them about your family. Tell them something about your background. Tell them what got you in the financial services. Tell them why you love doing what you do. If you have a great success story with a client—from either a previous employer or another branch of this bank, or from a referral you received from someone at this branch or in this room—tell it like a story so they get an idea of the kind of ways you can help people. Explain your process to them. But don't complicate how easy it can be to make a referral.

Referral Training: Where I Differ From the Whole Industry

Every product provider out there has a referral training piece or pieces. They all look the same. It's basically a one-pager: on one side is a list of thirty-five things to look for. On the backside is the script. Those are thirty-five things you are telling your bank employees to listen for when they interact with clients, and if any of those thirty-five subjects pop up—"REFER THE CLIENT TO ME!"

Yikes! The bank employee gets hives before they've even seen their next client—or they just completely give up before they start.

The thirty-five things approach rarely works from the bank employee's standpoint. It's just too overwhelming to remember. Most employees will be able to relate to perhaps five in total. Then, because they are distracted by their client's immediate requests, they forget those as well.

Employees and managers can send you 529 Plan referrals all day because that's the easiest referral for them. "I'm having a new baby, I'm having a new grandbaby, I'm worried about college funding."

Could you stay busy from sunup to sundown with 529s? Yes.

And then you'd go broke.

Instead of giving bank employees a list of thirty-five things to look for when speaking to clients, I give them two "R's" to look for:

1. *R*etirement-related matters.

2. *R*ate-related questions.

That's it. I'd rather have one retirement referral every day than fifty 529 referrals!

Psychologically, anyone can readily remember two to three items. If I give them the two most important things to look for, I'm more likely to get those referred to me. If I give them thirty-five things to look for, I am batting for zero referrals.

The heart of your business or where you make your money is *retirement planning*, whether it's pre-retirement or post-retirement.

That's where your money is. So I'd rather go for those. Okay, so your referral training tells the bank staff "anything retirement-related." Also, every time I say, "anything retirement-related," I follow up it with, "Oh, and by the way, the 'R' in IRA stands for retirement. All of those IRA clients should come see me first."

Next, we take anything *rate-related*. And you know at any given time you can usually beat the rates on bank deposit accounts. But more importantly, the rate-related questions are tied to money-in-motion: a CD coming due, an IRA rollover, or a high-balance liquid account.

The two R's—my "Just Two Things"—is my entire initial script for what bank frontline staff should focus on when looking for referrals. "Anything retirement-related, anything rate-related." (This last sentence might be your whole door-jamb training script some days.)

That is the heart of your referral training to bank staff. Experience tells me that out of a group, you'll have a couple of good referrers—people who have done it and are comfortable with it, or people who are naturally chatty with clients. A good referrer is also often somebody who's a little bit older and more comfortable with client interaction, or someone who is career-minded and determined to climb the corporate ladder. Treat those people like gold!

This, however, doesn't get everyone else off the hook. It doesn't mean we don't train everyone. Always be on the lookout for the next great referrer and remember how much employee turnover banks experience. At a minimum, everyone is capable of sending some referrals to you. If they see enough bank clients, they should at least have a few referrals fall into their lap.

From "Two R's" to "Two R's + Two D's'"

When an employee with a record of consistent referrals to you has become comfortable with rates and retirement, you can then add two more things: the two D's of death (in the family) and divorce. Print a picture of the Star Wars robot R2D2 and leave it on their desk while they are at lunch as a memory jogger.

Or you can personalize one referral source if you would be missing a really good opportunity. Maybe a big employer in the area often has long-tenured retirees or is infamous for mass lay-offs. Anything, in particular, that would be high gain activity and is easily identifiable. For example, if your branch is near a Boeing manufacturing plant or an Exxon refinery, a large number of your bank's customers probably work there. Those are the types of employers who may have long-tenured employees with generous retirement plans.

How Bankers Should Proceed With a Potential Referral

A frontline banker needs to know what to do when they identify a client of interest for you and how they get that client's information to you. How they proceed may vary widely from bank to bank.

It may be something as efficient and seamless as the employee sending you "an opportunity" through your CRM software tool, or it could be a Post-it note with a client's name and number that the employee sticks on your desk. Or, as I mention below, the employee might just walk with the client to your desk for that quick introduction if you are at their branch at the time. Usually, it's somewhere in between—like a form they fill out on the bank's intranet site. Regardless, you need to make sure they know how to get the referral to you, and therefore, you need to find out the bank's preferred procedure yourself! Then turn around and tell employees how to do this; if you don't train on this step, then your efforts are pointless.

An important part of educating a banker on how to proceed with a potential referral is the script you show them regarding what to say to the client or prospect.

The common script goes something like this:

"Have you met Doug Martinez? He's our financial advisor, licensed through XYZ broker-dealer. He helps people with retirement planning and income planning, and he can meet with you and build a financial plan that will help you reach all of your goals while incorporating all of your accounts and dreams and . . . ."

It's an eight to ten-line paragraph that the employee is supposed to memorize and repeat. But they never really memorize it, and when they try to say it, it comes out sounding like this:

"Do you know that we have a stockbroker here? His name is Doug. His office is over there, and if you want something long-term or if you're okay with something risky, he can help you out."

And then the client responds, "Yeah, yeah, you know, I think I'm good. I'll just stick with the CD."

Here are two different scripts *I* like. You can teach them both (because they are simple) or you can pick the one you like better.

1. "Have you met Ross Jones? He's our guy who helps people
    with that." Alternatively, "Have you met Juanita Smith?
    She's the best at helping people with that."

    Help is a good word. It's a power word. You know that people
    like to help other people. They like to receive help. Help is
    very benign. Nobody feels attacked when you say, "She can
    help you."

2. "Have you *thought about* doing something better?"

It's plain English, and it's not threatening. If the customer says, "No," then it's an easy response: "Well then, let me have Juanita give you a call."

In either scenario, the client may come back with a question of some sort:

"What would be better?"
"What's the rate?"
"Is it long-term?"

The frontline banker should never answer those questions. I repeat: never!

To *every question*, the frontline banker could just say this: "It sounds like you have some questions, so let me have Juanita give you a call. She's got the answers."

(An exception: it's okay for frontline bankers to answer the client if they ask a simple question, like, "Can I meet with her tomorrow?")

If there is no question posed, or they say they have not thought of doing better, then it's just this: "Let me have Ross Jones give you a call with that answer, and you can ask him anything else about it that comes to mind. He's your best person to talk to."

When I demonstrate this scripting in a training session in front of bank employees, I'll just say to one of them out of the blue, "What's your favorite kind of cookie?" I make it interactive in the group. The one I'm addressing says, "Chocolate chip." I say, "You know what's better?" And they'll say, "What?" And I'll say, "Hold that thought." I'll introduce this line in context of the referral: "Have you thought about doing something better?"

The fact about "better" is that it's "better than what the client now has." Even if you know your favorite cookie is chocolate chip, if I say, "Do you know what's better than chocolate chip?" You're going to say, "What kind of cookie is better?" You now have their attention.

If you happen to physically be in the branch, the employee can walk the client over to you for an introduction. Be sure to warmly thank the employee by name, right in front of the client, when he does that! The employee gets some public kudos, and the client is reassured that you know each other. (And the trust factor plus the branding factor get united in one easy interaction: "Thank you, Jenny! Have a seat, Mr. Smith!")

From the introduction onward, it's on you as the advisor to pursue the prospect and make a sale. That is about as warm a lead as anyone can ask for. And we don't really need any further profiling by the referrer because we have already narrowed down the kind of leads that are of the most value to us.

Giving Business Cards

A quick word on the old standby of giving the tellers and bankers a stack of business cards:

I would not go as far as saying this is a bad idea, but . . . it's sort of a bad idea.

I would guess the call-back rate on giving business cards is somewhere south of 1%. Even with the best intentions, people get busy and forget. It's nothing personal. I fear that giving frontline staff cards to give away might give them too easy of an "out." Giving a business card is easier than asking a question, so they may take the path of least resistance. Give them your contact information and keep it readily available so that they can call you with a prospect in front of them, ready to set an appointment. But let's not make it so easy that it will affect results.

We have to make it this simple, and it's not because the staff aren't smart. It's because they have fifteen things—or more!—on their plates. For most of them, their biggest concern is just making sure their drawer balances. This is an additional responsibility that we're putting on them. So we have to make it easy. Simple. Effortless. Comfortable. Straightforward.

Motivation

People are motivated by different things. Don't underestimate the value of finding their motivation. Your bank likely has some kind of token referral fee, maybe $10 to $20. You cannot rely on that to motivate. Most of them are not truly motivated by money. They may say they are, but even though it takes twenty seconds to make a referral for more than they usually make in an hour, most don't do it. Maybe one in five people actually do it with the money in mind.

A few other things you might consider:

- **Food.** Donuts at referral trainings are table stakes, but consider catering in lunch to a branch that has been productive.

- **Recognition.** Send a "Thanks for That Referral!" email to the referrer, copy the referrer's boss, and copy that boss's boss if possible. Some people just love being recognized. Another great opportunity for recognition is between branch managers. Talk about the top three branches on a branch manager call, or send out a monthly report of all branches, stack-ranking them by the most referrals. This tends to motivate people at the bottom just as well as people at the top!

- **Scorecards.** Understand how referrals help the employees' scorecards. Many banks have some sort of matrix that is used to determine job performance that can provide data for promotions or annual raises. This can be a big motivator for those looking to climb the career ladder in the bank.

- **Referral contests.** Some banks allow for them, and some don't, but if they're allowed, hold them—some people just like to win. More on that in a bit.

Keep Track

Remember how I insisted on formally keeping track of your *prospects, leads, and clients* and everything you've learned about them and done for them? Likewise, you'll want to use some system to track your *referrals* religiously—and those who sent them to you. Also, build a spreadsheet with a tab for every branch. List each employee. Know exactly where your referrals are coming from and how you can coach them up. I am not suggesting you try to be their sales manager, as we have no authority over them, but you can reward them accordingly and encourage and coach when something's not working.

When you have a good relationship with the referring employee, ask for a commitment in a casual way: "You think you can send me one referral next month?" That's not too much pressure, and you've gotten him thinking how he can do that. Then make note of commitments and follow up on them. With every referral, it gets easier for the frontline banker, but you also have to keep asking so your requests are top-of-mind.

I would guess you know exactly who your last five *client* referrals came from. But could you name exactly who your last *branch* referrals came from? Be sure you are doing follow-ups with referrers to let them know how the meetings went with the client they referred and share some real-life success stories of helping people. It gives them not only some success stories of their own to tell, but also confirmation that their referrals didn't disappear in a black hole.

Referral Contests

If your bank allows you to run referral contests, make sure you are getting the most out of them. The goal is to change short-term behavior in order to influence long-term behavior. Keep contests short. I think anything longer than a month gets forgotten. The last thing you want is to get to the end of a three-month contest and have the winner not know how or what they won. Set a minimum expectation—don't let anyone win a contest by sending only one referral!

I am not a fan of contests that involve drawings. Someone can work the hardest and still not win—that is demotivating. Be sure you are constantly promoting the contest. People forget, and if you aren't constantly promoting it, then you won't get the most out of it. And lastly, people love immediate gratification. Be ready to reward quickly.

The best referral contest I ever ran was simple. The *branch* that sent me the most referrals *each day* over a five-day workweek would get lunch catered in to the winner the next day, with a minimum of three referrals made to qualify for the contest. So Monday's winner got lunch on Tuesday, Tuesday's winner got lunch on Wednesday, etc. with Friday's winners being fed on Monday. I would send a few intraday emails to everyone giving live status updates to keep them engaged. They got immediate gratification, and it was very easy to understand the rules. It was a short enough period to hold attention. The prior day's winners were looked at with some envy and got everyone else moving! Then, the following week, I could call or visit each branch and say something like, "You sent me six referrals last Tuesday because you knew there was lunch on the line—do you think you could send me two this week?"

Branch Referral Advocates

This is a strategy, sometimes called Branch Referral Champions, that I have seen used with great success, and it's especially useful when you are covering a lot of branches. Designate one person in each branch as the Referral Advocate. This person is your eyes and ears in each branch, making sure that referrals are top of mind—someone to listen in on conversations and listen for referral and training opportunities.

Usually, this person is not the branch manager. (They're busy enough already.) Maybe you have a career-minded teller or a banker who is already good at giving referrals. This does not involve a raise or an official job title from the bank, and you may rotate the job from year to year. But it is a great opportunity to get someone some recognition that may have the capacity to contribute.

You can do Train the Trainer sessions with the Advocate, and they can pass it along for you. Do monthly conference calls and share results, making it a little competitive, and have them share best practices. Once a quarter, if geographically possible, get all the advocates together for a meal to reward and recognize. Between a nice meal and recognition, you will be surprised how people are eager to help.

You will not get every single bank employee engaged in promoting your business and sending you referrals. But you have to keep looking for the next great referrer, and you have to build bench strength for when you lose a good one. As one advisor said, "Find your twelve disciples." Then treat them like gold!

CHAPTER 4

ALL THE OTHER REFERRALS

In the preceding chapter, I showed you how to leverage the many frontline banking staff to build referrals for your business. In the banking environment, other bank employees with a great deal of minute-by-minute contact with clients can collect just enough information from each client to identify good prospects for you.

There are other ways of developing referrals that build your book of business. Keep in mind all cultivation is about people and relationships of trust. Which takes time. Using a referrals strategy well means you are committed to a long game. You are committed to your profession as a lifetime career.

Centers of Influence

Part of every advisor's business plan at some point in their career is to partner with COIs, or Centers of Influence. Wherever you were trained in the industry, you were more than likely told, "Go find lawyers and CPAs." And at some later point in our careers, we realized those people are never good sources of referrals!

One of the many advantages of being in the bank is that we have the opportunity to work with a whole other set of COIs. I am talking about *other bankers*. This is not the frontline staff, nor the branch managers, as they are always, always your target audience for the referral training you do on a regular basis.

By COI opportunities for bank advisors, I mean mortgage lenders, commercial bankers and lenders, merchant services sales reps, auto loan representatives, trust officers, senior management, and maybe even members of the board of directors (depending on your bank or credit union's size). Any other service that the bank offers probably has some people connected to it.

Reduce Perceived Risk

I talk a lot about getting the bank to like you and—most especially—to trust you. Trusting you with referrals means, even subconsciously to them, that you are not a risky bet. With all COI connections, this trust and minimal-to-no-risk perception are of utmost importance.

Be constantly aware that they are risking their relationships with their clients when sending them to you. These are relationships that they have built over years and years. If they refer someone to you who comes back to them saying, "Why did you send me to that clueless guy Alex?" they will *not* be sending any other referrals to you. They don't want their clients' trust in them to diminish due to a referral to you!

Long Development Period

Trust, like talents or skills, is not ever built in a day. In banks, we get very used to short sales cycles. This is very different. Plan for your development of COI referrals to be a very long sales cycle. It may take years to build relationships with commercial bankers, mortgage lenders, and other auxiliary services within the bank.

Not only do they have to trust that you aren't going to damage their relationship with their client, but they have to believe that you are making the right financial choices for their client. Your approach must always reflect that they deeply care about their clients.

Think about the way a wholesaler courts you. They take a genuine interest in your business. They're thoughtful, punctual, and professional. And they often try to have some fun with you.

Ponder this: there is a psychological response to eating with someone, to breaking bread with them. Take them to lunch or maybe a group dinner. Try to make some memories with them— invite them to play golf, see a baseball game, etc. Those things aren't just about quid pro quo as in, "I took you to have some fun, and now you owe me a referral." Yes, that may work, and you may get one, but imagine if a wholesaler had to take you to lunch every time they were hoping to get a trade!

Beyond the short-term gain, the long game is making memories and building a relationship. That takes time, and you can't force that in a genuine way. If they spend some time with you, they should hopefully get to like you.

Here are a few ideas to help you continue to build trust and promote professionalism, in no particular order:

- Provide economic updates or timely changes in your financial planning topics (much like you would for your "A" clients); conversely, ask for updates or changes to their business so that you can better refer to them.

- Review annual business plans with them.

- Set quarterly review meetings in advance.

- Invite them to client appreciation events (another opportunity to create memories) and let them see how you interact with clients. Give them two minutes of talk time to introduce themselves.

- Invite them to your client advocacy board events (see more on this interesting strategy in Chapter 5). These require a stepped-up level of professionalism, so it's a great opportunity to showcase your own interactions with clients.

Other sales professionals in the bank might also be good candidates to help you host your client advisory boards, but do not do that strictly to impress them. It will reflect on you and your business. Instead, do this only if you think they will do a good job and help you promote your brand. (More on branding your business in Chapter 6). Maybe they will learn something from that and ask you to host a client advocacy board for them. That would give you the opportunity to become valuable in their business, too!

Reality Check

I am realistic and experienced enough to know that many bank advisors will not do any of this. Many can make a good living without it—true. It's not something that all the large producers do—true. But the fact is there are many very, very large producers who have built their businesses *entirely through doing this*. Many of the strategies we are discussing in this book apply primarily to retail bank advisors, but advisors in commercial banks will generally be using this as their sole strategy to meet clients.

Social Networking

This is not about social media, but about club-type organizations you attend in person. I meet a lot of people who join, join, join. They are at the Chamber of Commerce, Kiwanis Club, Rotary Club, Lions Club, and the other big, visible social or professional organizations in town.

Financial advisors are no exception: they attend all meetings and events and might even be officers to gain further visibility. The problem is that they are spending their time and efforts doing this because they aren't doing what it takes to meet prospects in the bank. They are not meeting people there, where they work—either because they don't know how to properly leverage the bank system through the types of strategies and tactics I present in this book, or because they have gone through the motions and it's just not working, for whatever reason.

I say this: if you want to do the social networking because you enjoy volunteering or just relaxing and rubbing shoulders with other professionals of the city, then go for it. I'm a member of one club myself and enjoy it immensely. But you should not *have* to do it to find prospects. If that is the only way you are meeting prospects, then you should go independent and get a higher compensation payout. If you want to do it because you *like it*, that's your choice.

Personally, when I was an advisor, I was a member of the Kiwanis Club. While they knew I worked for a bank, no one ever knew I was a financial advisor, and I kept things that way on purpose. That was my preference. Kiwanis events were my time away from the office just to be social with other professionals of the city. I took off my financial advisor hat. I'm not saying that's the right thing to do with such a social networking opportunity, but that's what I enjoyed.

Many of the top producers I talk to promote themselves outside of the office—no doubt, and more power to them. But they do it while also engaging in activities they really, truly enjoy doing—playing golf, volunteering, doing family activities, etc. These social occasions are never their primary means of finding clients.

And by the way, if you want to use social networking as a business building strategy, be sure to read about and deeply, carefully ponder your brand (more in Chapter 6)! At social networking events, you'll need that fifteen-second branding pitch to answer the question "What do you do for a living?"

Client Referrals

Many top producers rely heavily on client referrals for a significant portion of their business. There are at least three reasons they are able to do that:

1. **Their client base is quite large.** When a modest percentage of their clients are willing and able to refer new contacts to them, that presents a large pool of potential new business. You will never have a huge percentage of clients that send referrals, so to some degree, it's a numbers game.

2. **They play the long game.** That is, these advisors have relationships that they hold on to and nurture over time. They prove themselves over a long period of time to their clients. Thus, clients are very comfortable referring others "like them" to the advisor.

3. **Some are now book brokers, no longer working the branch network.** Client referrals are their only way to gain new clients, so they put more effort into securing them.

The reality is that client referral flow is just never what you hope it will be. Increasingly, getting client referrals is one of the most common questions and challenges I hear. Advisors know that client referrals hold, by far, the greatest capability for quick new clients because of the built-in trust. If this is a goal, ask yourself what specific actions you're taking to gain those referrals. Build it into your marketing plan. This is not the time to become complacent! Based on my conversations with advisors who see the best results, they go out and get those referrals.

Here are the easiest ideas for developing a referral pipeline from your current clients:

Develop client advisory boards and hold regular lunch or dinner meetings consistently. (See that full approach in Chapter 5.) Hold client appreciation events that include a "bring a friend" invitation. (See how that works in Chapter 15.)

Any time you hold these events, be sure you say to the group, "I would like to thank those of you who have sent me referrals." Say this systematically and with sincere gratitude at each and every event, *even when* you know that no one present has given you a referral. Make them feel like they should be doing so. Make them think, every time they meet with you, that they may be the only ones who have not referred "someone just like them" to you. Notice, I say, "just like them," because if you properly apply a branding statement, then the referral should be natural, if not obvious.

Go back to all the old ideas you may have heard in training as an insurance agent or wirehouse advisor. Say, perhaps, you hear your client mention that they are in a sewing circle. What do you do? You offer to host the sewing circle's holiday luncheon at a nice restaurant. Say that you learn that one of your clients is an avid golfer. What do you do? You tell them to pick six buddies, and you take them to a course they wouldn't normally play.

You might have to spend your own money, which most bank advisors are not accustomed to. You can ask your bank to help, but it is just not common to get that support. Alternatively, you can talk to wholesalers who might help out; most would prefer to invest in your business than just go out to dinner. The return on investment is evident: if you buy lunch for six prospects in a low-pressure, fun way with an introduction from a current client, maybe you spend $150. My guess is you have a good chance at getting at least one or two meetings from it. Let's say you get one trade. What are your average trade size and average gross commission? The numbers work.

Circle Back to Trust

Learning about and getting comfortable with people is a key to garnering more trust. Trust is the most important trait in earning referrals to your financial advisory business.

I get it: some of these approaches and tactics might not be of interest to you. Or they might be out of your comfort zone right now. Nonetheless, be sure to choose one by the time you have finished this book. Start small and build one or two business-building strategies into your business plan. Be tactical, be creative, and be willing to try something new.

CHAPTER 5

CLIENT ADVOCACY BOARDS

This chapter could also be called: One Last Source of Referrals. Here's part of what I mean: once you have turned a prospect into a client, you should solidify your relationship with that client so that they 1) return to you again and again with their own new needs over the long term, and 2) are willing to refer "people just like them" to you, people who also become your clients.

Here's the other part of what I mean: creating client advocacy boards is one terrific way to achieve both of these primary goals. And yes, you read correctly—not only a single board, but *boards*. You may have heard them called client advisory boards. Call it what you want, but as you will see, we want your clients *advocating* for your business.

Invite Your Clients onto an Advocacy Board

Advocacy equals referrals.

"Advocating" means promoting and speaking out in favor of you, your knowledge, and your business.

Being on your board—especially someone who has always believed that "being a board member" only happens in big corporations or is only open to the rich and widely influential individual—makes your client feel special. They can say to their friends with pride, "I'm going to my board meeting," and that is somewhat of a prestigious thing. Also, feeling special makes them alert to their role on the board for you; they'll want to rise to those obligations for you. They will take an interest in your business and want to see you succeed. And, as an extra perk for you, rarely will a client fire their financial advisor if they are on their own advisor's board!

Having this client on your board strengthens your relationship with them by demonstrating that you are not just transactional or once-and-done in your advisory role with them. You're in it for the long term. This long-term perspective opens up in the client's mind more ways you can serve them in their financial needs.

Get Referrals

Referrals, as I've been saying in many different ways, are the lifeblood of your business. The second goal is having the board help you get referrals from your current (and now board member) client. They are more inclined to "talk you up" to family, colleagues, and friends when they see firsthand how well you are treating them and how you value their input and point of view. Being part of the board will give them the words they need to talk you up as well!

A Third Goal

By creating and leading client advocacy boards, you create an opportunity to solicit and collect ideas from your board members—ideas that will help you run a better business.

Periodically, you will also be asking your board to give you feedback on how you're doing for them. We live in a service economy, and—let's face it—people who are service consumers will always have an opinion about what you did right and what you did blatantly wrong. People are usually open to offering suggestions about how you can improve.

You can formalize the feedback process with a printed questionnaire. I include sample questions at the end of this chapter to inspire you. Having prepared questions tells the board members that you are serious about their guidance, and that will lead them to reflect and give more complete, thoughtful responses. Additionally, you will have a record of that advice for you to refer back to for your progress. Keep the questions at a high level (no diving deep into the weeds and details) and see what your clients have to share.

When you do this sort of "service audit questionnaire" with each of your boards, you will also, hopefully, see trends. The trends over time may be things that all clients are looking for but that you are not addressing in your advice to them. I would suggest you set reasonable expectations, as we know clients may suggest things that we cannot follow through on.

Build Your Business With Many Client Advocacy Boards

If you are unsure of the success of this tactic, I should tell you that I work with an advisor who does this very regularly. As a matter of fact, he has been building his entire business using these client advocacy boards. Read that again: *this is the only business-building and referral-collecting tactic he employs.* The bank he works in has very little local presence. He gets no support. Hopefully, you don't find yourself in this situation, but... know that it can work.

Every time he accumulates twelve new clients, he creates a new board and invites all twelve to be members! They have no idea that he is creating a new board every month with twelve other new clients. He is just living off the referrals that come from current board members and clients.

I might also mention that he is consistently the top producing advisor in his firm. He makes a *ton* of money just creating and facilitating client advocacy boards. He is a good financial advisor and came to the realization that this would be the one and only way he'd be identifying new prospects and gaining new clients for his business, given his situation.

How to Invite Clients to Be Board Members

Select a group of current clients—ideally not more than ten or twelve individuals for each board. This could be five or six couples or a combination of couples and single/widowed/divorced individuals. You could do as this advisor did and simply invite the twelve newest clients and hope that the group is diverse and interesting. Or, especially if you now have a book of clients, you can mix them up to form any type of board you wish.

The invite is a simple phone call:

"Mr. Client, hello. This is _____, your financial advisor at Bank XYZ. I hope you're doing well today. I am calling with an invitation for you (and your spouse) and to ask you a special personal favor."

"You know I take a great amount of pride in running my business and doing a great job for my clients. I'm putting together a luncheon for what I call a client advocacy board (*for credit unions, member advisory board*). I'm basically looking for feedback and suggestions so that I can better run my business for my best clients like you, and I'd like you to be part of that."

"We're planning on having a lunch meeting next month on Wednesday the 18th at 11:30 a.m., and I would like you to join me and a few other clients for lunch at The Main Street Grill restaurant. I can email you the details so you have them in writing, but do you think you can make it?"

Event Agenda

Let the new board members know in advance what is on the agenda of the first board meeting, so there is no trepidation or discomfort.

Enjoy a nice lunch (or dinner, if you're targeting clients who are still working) to thank them for their business and to thank them for offering their opinions so you may better serve them and the community. Just like client appreciation events, which you'll read about later, the restaurant venue doesn't have to be expensive. It should be nice enough that they look forward to the meal but not so nice that they would only come for the free meal. I would specifically suggest looking for a restaurant that has a back room that can be closed off, or a section they typically don't use during the lunch hour, if you are hosting over lunch.

Allow some socializing time . . . then get down to business. Your introduction:

"We want to thank you for coming and taking a few minutes to enjoy a nice lunch. We appreciate that you are willing to give us a little feedback in hopes of helping me serve you bet-ter. I would like to introduce _____ (*any business partners or guests*). We are going to order lunch, and that will give us a few minutes to chat and get to know each other a little. As we wrap up lunch, we will go through some questions and have a little conversation. We should have you out of here by _____ o'clock."

To spark conversation, throw out softball questions to get people talking. Ask how you could run your business for current clients—"How often would you like to hear from me?"—and be cautious of not overpromising on standards that you can't fulfill. Then sprinkle in a couple of client acquisition questions: "Would you feel comfortable referring your friends or family?" or "Does the topic of 'who is your financial advisor?' ever come up?" You can use the questions to prime the conversation, but in my experience, once people start opening up, it goes very well.

An option that some advisors employ is having a co-host ask the questions without the advisor in the room. I have done this for several advisors, and it seems to be well received. They know their feedback about me is anonymous; I won't know who made which comment. Interestingly, feedback tends to be very positive. I have not had a client bad-mouth an advisor in this scenario. In doing this, you want to be sure you are partnering with someone you know and trust, someone who would represent your business well. As I tell my kids, you are judged by the company you keep. But I do think it's a good move to show your clients that you are genuinely interested in their feedback. Co-hosts could be wholesalers (especially when asking them to pay), sales managers, senior bank management, or other COIs in the bank—mortgage lenders, commercial lenders, etc.

End each board meeting with a subtly-worded request for referrals. Say, "I am here at Bank XYZ to serve people just like you, people you know who might need sound financial advice. Just let me know who you need me to talk with. Thanks for coming today—and most importantly, thank you for the referrals that you have already given me." Again, you express gratitude, even if you know that none have yet to give you a referral!

As you see, the advocacy board has two real objectives: 1) improve your business, approach, presentations, etc. through commentary your own clients make to you, and 2) earn referrals.

Follow Up

You cannot seriously expect to improve your business (and build the trust of those board members) in viable ways unless you truly examine and act upon recommendations made to you on the service audits. Ask your co-host to compile the feedback results and spend time debriefing. Devise your own action plan to do one or more of those recommended suggestions. Later, you can go back to the board for further comments on how you've been doing at that new suggestion!

For any such meeting, if you can walk away with two to three actionable items, you have been successful. It doesn't hurt to call each attendee and again thank them for joining. With any luck, maybe the topic of referrals comes up again. Seize the opportunity to confirm that client referrals are both desired and welcomed—even expected—from your clients.

Sample Questions for Your Feedback "Service Audit" Distributed to Board Members

- Why did you choose me as your financial advisor?

- Have I met, exceeded, or fallen below your expectations?

- What one aspect do you feel I should improve on?

- Is there one aspect you feel I do exceedingly well?

- Am I communicating with you enough and in a timely fashion?

- Have I done a good job in conveying my full array of services to you?

- Do you have any comments about the strengths or weaknesses of my competitors?

- How often would you like to be contacted?

- Are there any value-added services you would suggest I add to my practice?

- What one aspect would make you consider using a different financial advisor than me?

- Are you aware that I offer the following products and services? (Check if "yes"):
  - ☐ Retirement Planning
  - ☐ Life Insurance
  - ☐ Long-Term Care Insurance
  - ☐ Education Funding
  - ☐ Estate Planning

- Number the following in order of importance to you (1 = most important, 5 = least important)
  - ☐ Return/Performance
  - ☐ Staff/Group Size
  - ☐ Technology
  - ☐ Service/Response Time
  - ☐ Variety of Products Available

CHAPTER 6

A DIFFERENTIATING BRAND

L isten, I know you have been to conferences or listened to webinars and heard enough about branding. But the fact is that not enough advisors employ this easy opportunity to differentiate their services in such a direct way. You can't change my mind about that because I have seen it work.

Over the years, I have asked many financial advisors, "What is your brand?" and the answer is some five-second variation of "full-service financial planning" or "holistic financial planning."

Sorry, but that's not your brand. It might be what you do all day, but it is definitely not your *differentiator.*

The other kind of answer I get is some variation of a thirty-second elevator speech. That also is usually not your brand. That is just more of what you do and what you offer and perhaps how you do it.

Don't get me wrong. You need that five-second response and that thirty-second elevator pitch. You will always have an opportunity to use them. *But they need to express your brand.*

Your brand is a statement that differentiates you from all the rest of the financial advisors any one of your prospective clients has talked to.

Think of a brand that sparks an emotion in you. If you possess the Zippo lighter that your grandfather carried in WWII and that your father later carried in Vietnam, Zippo is a brand that sparks an emotion in you. If I asked you to tell me about Zippo lighters, you might have an emotional response. You might even tear up.

What you definitely *wouldn't* say? "They light cigarettes." Or, "It's just a pocket lighter brand I carry around." What you would do, because Zippo lighters have—for you and your family— differentiated themselves from every other type, is *tell me a story.* And let me say that *once I hear your story,* I'm not going to forget it!

I am not suggesting that anyone asking your clients about you would make your clients get emotional, but what you don't want them to say is "He does full-service financial planning." Yawn. So what? What does that mean, anyway?

My question about defining your brand is a simple one to ask, but not always simple to answer.

Here's What Your Brand Really Is

Let's say your client is at a cocktail party talking to friends, and the topic of financial advisors comes up. Someone says to your client, "Tell me about your financial advisor."

What will that client say? Is that the same as what you would *hope* they say?

As financial professionals, we are selling an intangible, a service. Branding is describing, defining, drawing a picture, creating a mental image about that intangible. Branding in that way turns your intangible service into a picture that they can understand much more readily.

Your brand helps you identify to all your leads and prospects what you are "selling" and what you do for them, so that the most qualified prospects will ultimately seek out your services. Since the brand has served to qualify them—that means fitting the profile of your ideal client—you can quickly and easily get on the same page with the prospect and turn them into a client.

You have to not only live your brand but also communicate it to your prospects and clients, so they will do business with you and then communicate it to others who need what you do. You need to be able to finish the following two statements—perhaps in a few ways each—and you must repeat this as appropriate so that people know what you are about:

1. People hire me because ...

2. The reason to stop looking is ...

If you can't state these answers, your prospects or clients cannot determine whether or not you're the obvious choice. And I am sure you know this goes without saying, but it can't be related to a *product*. It absolutely can be related to a *process* because everyone has the same products.

There is, perhaps, value to you to leverage the bank's or credit union's brand as part of yours, by thinking about what it was about the bank's or credit union's brand that attracted the client in the first place. (Or even you, when you were looking for a bank to practice your profession.)

- If you work in a national brand bank, maybe what drew those clients in was the convenience, great technology, and a branch on every corner. Maybe it was the security of a nationally known, century-old name. Think seriously about the convenience factor of your brand. Ponder the weightiness and implicit trustworthiness of a long-established brand.

- If you work at a regional or "non-household name" bank or a smaller one with no particular name recognition, it might have been the exclusivity, the specialization, or the attraction of a personal touch of that smaller size that drew the client in.

- If you are in a small credit union or community bank, there is a good chance that clients chose it because they value a bank that knows their industry (in the case of an industry-specific credit union), provides personalized service, or has staff who know them by name.

When you have a pretty good hint at what is already making them buy, leverage that by providing more and more of whatever it was that drew the client to the bank.

Your Brand Must Resonate

Let me tell you how several advisors I know developed their brand and continue to leverage it every day to develop their book of business.

I know an advisor in East Texas, in a small, conservative community. His brand, as he explained to me in our first conversation, is one short statement:

"I am the safe money expert."

If someone wants something safe, he is their guy. It doesn't mean he doesn't use equities, but when he does, he errs on the side of conservative. He tells people, "If you want the next hot stock or you are expecting double-digit returns every year, I am not your guy. I help you grow your money, and we play it safe based on how much risk you can handle."

He knows that in conservative East Texas, this is a brand that will resonate. He may lose some prospective clients, but not many. His branding does the qualifying for him: if the younger or high-risk-tolerant prospect is "not into safe right now," they do not qualify as one of his ideal clients (from his perspective), and he doesn't qualify as their best advisor (from the client's perspective). It works for him in his context, for his style, and his target market's needs. His brand? *Safe money guy.*

I know another top producer whose credit union is associated with the shipyard that does government contracts for the U.S. Navy. The shipyard has had several owners over the last twenty-plus years—big companies that you would associate with the aerospace, defense, and security industries. Employees may have as many as four different versions of the pension depending on when they started working at the shipyard and who owned it at the time. It's very complicated and there's a ton of paperwork involved.

But the advisor, as an outsider, learned every rule and nuance of *all* the pensions and *all* the retiree healthcare programs. He mastered them to the degree that when the shipyard's employee who was tasked with helping others process their retirement paperwork himself retired, his position was not backfilled. Why not? As the next waves of people retired, they were just sent straight to the advisor for clarification and help. His brand? *Expertise in the shipyard employees' retirement and healthcare options—all of them—and leveraging them to help each and every employee retire with peace of mind.*

I know another advisor who served mostly engineers in an area near technology laboratories in the New Mexico desert. We have all worked with engineers—and feared it!—and we know how they want to work. They want to know how the sausage is made. This is as much a relationship sale as it is a sale of details, facts, alphas, betas, and capture ratios. They are smart clients, and they expect a smart advisor.

This financial advisor was able to be that smart one for them. By narrowing his focus on the breadth of products that he offered (more on this later) and focusing on developing and sharing a real depth of knowledge on his offerings, he captured the engineering population's trust and respect, and by extension, that of all the staff members working in those companies. If his clients wanted to know every quantitative measure of their investments, he had the ready answers. He was known as an analytical, albeit outgoing advisor who could go toe-to-toe with some of the smartest engineers in the country.

Anecdotally, I asked him how he would articulate his brand for my purpose of writing this book. He said, "I'm kind, I'm smart, and I'm beautiful." This is what I deal with. He said that. But notice the *realism* in his self-description: he's kind (likable); he's smart (meeting the client's expectations); he's a charming and wonderful individual (a pleasure for clients to meet and work with). His brand, in my words? *I'm kind and likable, and I speak your analytical language.*

Look again at how the context of environment helped each of the above advisors determine their brand. What's your community or context? (Conservative, like the East Texas advisor? One big employer in town? One type of professional in town? Some other definitive trait?) How does your community or context help you develop your brand and reach your clientele?

Branding's Bottom Line

As my friend and mentor Don Connelly once told me (and no one knows more about soft-selling skills than Don):

"When Ma and Pa get back in the car after meeting with you, neither one says, 'What did you think of that *upside capture ratio*, honey?' Pa says, 'What did you think of that advisor fella, Mama?'"

You still have to be likable and trustworthy. You still have to communicate and listen well. But if a prospect's financial concerns and personal values align with your brand, you will have a huge leg up in not only winning *them*, but winning referrals from their friends and family who are just like them.

Now over to you. I can't tell you what your brand is or what your branding statement should be. I can tell you that you need to have one. It has to contain *differentiators*. This is your opportunity to stand out in the sea of sameness. You have to be able to communicate it clearly and quickly.

Not every advisor is going to be a "safe money guy." Not all of us are going to specialize in "guaranteed income for your entire retirement." Not all of us are going to be in a niche-market bank or industry location. Examine what it is that is different for your practice of this profession.

Brand Equation

Use what I call your brand equation, which should be a combination of these five things. This can help you develop your brand.

1. Why are you in the business?

    This is your personal *Why*. Why are you in this business? Why is this your passion? Why are you with the company you are with?

2. What do you enjoy doing?

   Say you define your brand as a "safe money expert," and you find yourself talking to prospects and clients often about fixed annuities—because that is how you've set your business up. That is fine for some, but not if your *passion* is constructing equity portfolios. You are going to lose your mind talking about that all day. Likewise, if you don't have an encyclopedic memory, the tech-lab-engineering type of client will make you sweat bullets during every appointment you have. You get the idea.

3. What are your clients already buying via their banking relationship?

   Consider the individuals who are already clients of your bank. Why are they with that bank? I've brought this up before, but re-examine it now: is it the convenience or brand name of the big national bank you work in? The personal touch and relationships of the community bank? The relationship your credit union has with a local employer? Advanced technology?

4. What should clients be buying?

   In my example of the advisor in New Mexico, the engineers from the tech labs generally had pensions so rich they all had a surplus at the end of the month. He, therefore, knew that a "lifetime guaranteed income" conversation was wasted breath! That fact helped determine his brand and was why he focused on growth and wealth transfer matters.

5. What opportunities surround you? (Consider geography, demographics, large employers, etc.)

Is your area similar to that of my East Texas advisor— very conservative? Or are you in a more fast-paced coastal environment? What are the characteristics of the largest employer in your region? Is there only one or are there many in one industry, like the New Mexico advisor has? How should that play into developing your brand to that market?

Put those five things together, and you will have your brand. The weighting of each factor's importance will vary from one person and case to the next. Try out a few statements of your brand until it feels right. Write down how you will communicate your brand, so you know the script. Trust your gut, but also trust the numbers. There is a Law of Large Numbers aspect to sales that says, "If you have enough repetitions, you can measure if your statement is working or not." Don't stop measuring at the first transaction, of course . . . but we will get to that soon.

Your brand is what other people say about you
when you're not in the room.
—Jeff Bezos

Part Two

MAKING THE SALE

The financial planning process is largely the same for many in the profession, no matter the channel we work through: bank advisors, wirehouses, insurance companies, RIAs, independent advisors. We use the same products and often the same financial planning software, and we help clients reach the same types of goals.

The big difference between all those channels and the bank environment is clear: bank customers are not usually walking in the branch specifically looking for a financial advisor. They are walking in to cash or deposit checks, make payments, replace a worn-out ATM card, and so on. They may not even be aware that the bank employs a financial advisor. And some (many!) may not be able to say what such an advisor does.

One way we are different from other channels is that often we have to, at least initially, be to the client what they want us to be to them. And that is *not* a financial advisor!

Many wirehouse advisors set out with the goal of finding one hundred clients with at least a million dollars in investable assets. They will end up with $100–$300 million under management, and most of it will be in fee-based accounts. That will make for a pretty good living. If you work for a large bank in a large city, or you are with a private banking group, that may work for you, too.

However, for the vast majority of bank advisors, this doesn't work. First, most of our clients fall into the "mass affluent" market, meaning they possess $250,000–$750,000 in investable assets. Not that you won't find the million-dollar client from time to time. You might! But if you specifically set out with that business model in mind, you'll be heading down a very long and slow road.

Additionally, I should add that if you tell the bank staff to only send you those clients with a million dollars in assets or net worth, they will think you are a snob, and you will never get referrals from them. That's even truer in a credit union environment.

This lesser investable asset position of your clients is important because it makes for a different sales model. When their client walks into their Merrill Lynch office, both parties know exactly what they are going to talk about. When a client walks into the local bank branch where you are the financial advisor, they aren't necessarily looking for you at all.

Often, while your bank customers are not looking for a financial planner, they are looking for help or will accept help on a piece of money. Perhaps they are aware that their CD has come due. They feel they have too much money in a liquid account. Or they might need help moving an old retirement plan. This can lead to a very transactional business with you. There are a lot of bank advisors who may have 1,000 clients, but those 1,000 clients have only bought one product from them. That's transactional.

Since the business's inception, much is made of the transactional relationship versus the planning relationship. Every sales manager has the goal every year of pushing advisors to a more planning-based model. But even the most planning-based advisors—the ones who love to crank out their eighty-seven-page output—will tell you that they honestly do plans for about only 10%–20% of their clients.

A hallmark of top producers that I'll call to your attention is that they use *transactional* business as a way to grow their *planning* business. Sometimes it's prospecting for the whale and to identify those clients who are open to a more rigorous planning relationship. But there are advisors who gross well over a million dollars, and their business is really just a series of transactional trades.

The moral of the story is that you have to make a sale. *You should strive to make a sale every day.*

That is a different mindset for many. Some independent advisors who find their way to the bank channel are not used to having appointments every day. *You need to be conducting multiple appointments every day, and you should be making sales every day.*

I don't mean just moving someone down the path to buying something, although you do have to do that. I mean you should be closing on something every day. To do that, your sales process has to be predictable, repeatable, and, most importantly, simple.

The biggest-producing advisors who I meet have the simplest sales process. They use a small number of carefully selected investment options, and their close ratio is very close to 100%. They *assume* people are going to buy. And it doesn't come across as cocky by any means. It's confidence in the idea that if a client presents a goal or a set of needs to you, and you correctly understand those goals and needs, and then you present a proper recommendation to fulfill those goals and needs—well, there's no reason why the client wouldn't act on it. Further, there is no reason that the client wouldn't act on it *immediately.*

Another hallmark of large-producing bank advisors is that they are continuously transitioning the transactional customer into deeper relationships. *This might be the biggest shortfall of the average-producing bank advisor.* You get busy, you get another referral, someone else walks in the door, you get covered in a mountain of paperwork . . . you've fallen into the trap of acting busy. You may not even have entered this transactional client into your business prospect-tracking software. That means that you never really get back to those people who are in fact now your clients, to build on that initial relationship, find the rest of their assets, and do more in-depth planning with them.

The chapters in this section will help you put more thought into a very purposeful, scripted, and scalable sales process. But you allow them to buy in the way that they want to buy.

We are all chasing the same clients and the same dollar with the same investments. In my eyes, how you communicate in making the sale determines who will get the money.

Consider Basic Communications

Here are a few tips based on what I see from the more successful advisors. New advisors or advisors aiming for higher productivity should adopt them.

1. **Talk less.** I know you are mouthing the words "that's not me" while you roll your eyes. But it might be you. The top producers are selective and impactful with their words. They aren't big talkers. Further, if you want someone to like you more, you talk less. Why? So they can talk about themselves, which is what people love to do. It's not that these advisors won't carry on a conversation or aren't social. But if you're like me, if you keep talking, you will eventually say something dumb. And lose the sale.

2. **Simplify.** I tell advisors to simplify it to the level you need to, so that your client or prospect will understand—and then, simplify it again. Don't use big words and don't use industry terms. Just plain English. Please see that this is not being condescending to them! By talking over their head, you may get an account, but you won't get the rest of their money. And you certainly will not get a referral from them.

3. **Practice specificity.** Most people speak in generalities. Be as specific as possible (without using too many words and without complicating it). In your referral training with bank staff, an example of how to be simple and specific is this: "The 'R' in IRA stands for retirement, and all of those people would benefit from meeting with me."

4. **Sell with stories.** You already know this. But it works. Look up Nick Murray and Don Connelly. No one sells with stories better.

CHAPTER 7

YOUR PRODUCT MENU

Trust is the foundation for your business relationships and business-building success. Examine how *preparation*—or the lack thereof—either supports or sabotages that trust-building effort. Preparation starts with your formal training, certainly, closely followed by your understanding of the products you sell. How well can you present and distinguish each product right now? That is the question!

Preparedness Equals Confidence

Consider this scenario:

A client walks into your office. You listen and ask a few questions. You determine that given the circumstances or problem or goal the client presents to you, the client needs a tax-free municipal bond fund. That is the product that best fits his needs as he expresses them to you.

If the client needs a tax-free bond fund from you, that is what they get. Not something else. From your thorough preparation, you should know exactly what tax-free bond fund to use when a client needs one—you know the distinctions among the funds. Then you present that to the client. You know the current yield. You know the expense ratio. You know the performance history. You also know that if you have a *minor* question or confusion that the wholesaler will pick up your call, even if it's 8 p.m.

The keyword in my last statement is "*minor.*" What you don't do in this scenario is call six fund companies, in front of the client, and ask what their current yield is. Current yield and six calls are *major*! Neither do you fumble around on a website trying to find literature (that you should already possess), nor ask the client to wait while you do a real-time numbers check . . . or whatever other line you come up with to cover your lack of preparedness.

You want your prospect or client to feel assured that you have done this many, many times before. You achieve this impression through complete preparation on all your products. They need to see and hear that you have exact and ready information available to you and them. They get very nervous when their need, their request, their account looks like an experiment, and you seem like an intern. Familiarity and preparation on your part breed confidence on their part.

We Are Not a Product Business

This might seem to contradict what I have just said and will also be saying next. It does not. Ask yourself, "What business am I in?" While we certainly need products to solve problems, we are in the people business. Our goal is to give people financial peace of mind by solving problems they feel they are experiencing. (And hint, hint—this could figure into your branding, right?)

Getting caught up in constantly researching products is a rookie mistake. One of the keys to scaling your business is simplification—creating repeatable processes—and this includes product *selection*.

Apart from the simplification it offers you in processing business and servicing your book of business, product menu simplification most importantly creates a repeatable process in your presentations. If you have told the story of each product fifty times, your presentation will be much better than if you have only presented it twice. You know the questions the client will ask. You are ready for even the toughest objections and answer them before the client can voice them.

You do have to build a shelf. While you may have literal shelves of product literature, I am speaking of a metaphorical "product shelf": the arrows in your quiver or the tools in your toolbox. I am not going to tell you what to sell, but the fact is that products are involved in what we do. *Which* products are a personal decision based on a lot of factors (hint: it again involves your branding and the answer to what business you are in), but I am going to tell you that you have to build a shelf. Keep this in mind: it's a shelf, not a carousel.

We have a responsibility to our clients to make appropriate recommendations. We do not have the responsibility to constantly be chasing down the next best thing.

Within one product type, how many different options do you really need? Variable annuities are an example. You probably just need one. Maybe you need two, possibly three options if there are differentiating factors, but I encourage you not to use more.

Again, one of the goals of your business is *simplification*, and that includes the number and types of products on your shelf. If you are new in the business or not seeing a lot of prospects yet at the bank you've just joined, you might feel like you have time to:

- Meet with multiple wholesalers.

- Research products.

- Do required product training.

- Learn multiple agent codes for many companies.

- Stay abreast of product changes and performance.

- Keep updated literature.

- Learn servicing nuances of each company.

Wrong! You will not get to bigger production numbers constantly doing those things.

You should select, learn, and know your small product menu perfectly.

Some products should be avoided. These are my personal beliefs about what not to have in your product selection:

- **No brokered traditional CDs.** People don't always understand the mark-to-market pricing, and I think you stand more to gain by referring that money back to the bank, although you have to then humbly publicize that you are referring money back to the bank. Remember to track maturities on this money that you refer back and consider it assets under administration.

- **No individual stocks.** The exception is ACAT transfers of current positions to consolidate accounts. Researching, recommending, and being available to trade individual stocks is just not the business we are in. We are not "stockbrokers." I know it's exciting, but you'll waste valuable time in the researching, it can ruin a relationship, and you will make no money in the process. If someone says they want individual stock, tell them to open an online brokerage account with their fun money and reiterate to them that you want to help them with their serious money.

Build your shelf. Focus on products you find easy to explain and understand. If you find them easy, so will clients. Here's a sample product menu:

- 1–2 fixed annuities

- 1–2 indexed annuities

- 1 registered indexed annuity

- 1–2 variable annuities (assuming they have differentiating benefits)

- 1 REIT company

- 1 UIT company

- 2 mutual fund families (with different strengths)

- 1 managed money platform (there may be a handful of strategies you use—and not more than a handful)

That's all you need. That's what a top producer would put on his own shelf. When you have decided on a shelf with something like the above selection of products, you select which carriers to use.

Lose One, Gain One

There is a slow evolution of products, and that means a time commitment from you for staying informed as products do evolve, but you can be methodical about it. Be thorough and do the research for yourself, understand the benefit to your client, but also know the benefit to you (as that will be part of your book of business). You will field questions and be held accountable for performance and servicing the account.

Over time, and for every new product added to the shelf, one product must be taken down. From time to time, you may have to create a new slot, but the idea is to keep the shelf the same size over the long term. This also means that when you meet with a wholesaler, they have to tell you a convincing enough story for you to take one of your other products off the shelf.

Master your products through a wise, small selection of them and thorough preparation on each of them. That helps with the next step: mastering your transactional sales.

CHAPTER 8

MASTERING THE TRANSACTIONAL SALE

If people walked into the bank looking for a financial advisor, the job would be easy. It also probably wouldn't pay very well.

I would guess that not many of your prospects have said, "Please tell me about mutual fund and annuity options." I often joke that when people walk into the bank and say they would like to buy equities, that means it's time to short the market. (That's not real investment advice—don't do that!)

There are certainly advisors who have built their business just looking for clients who are seeking out or are immediately open to a traditional advisor/client relationship. I am not going to spend a lot of time outlining how to solicit a traditional advisor/client relationship because you probably focused on those at a brokerage firm or insurance company before you came to the bank. There are a lot of books and resources available on that topic, too.

The fact is that most people come to a bank with a *transactional* mindset, the same way they would open a CD or apply for a car loan. They want to walk in, talk to someone, make a decision, and walk out.

Here Is a Hint

When you embrace transactional business as a way to grow and a step into relationship-building mode, you will possess a business-building tactic that works very well.

Let me give you my definition of transactional business. This is our common client: someone comes in to solve a problem or to have you address one piece of money and not "the bigger picture." It does not mean a specific product, because it could be an annuity, a retail mutual fund, or even managed money. Transactional business in the bank may or may not be fee-based, but the point is you are not doing comprehensive planning or gathering assets (yet). You are just starting with one transaction. In this way, financial advisors in banks end up working a lot like emergency room doctors. We solve a problem and send them on their way.

First, look at the value and benefits of the transactional sale. When you take care of a client's transactional needs, this:

- brings in immediate assets and commissions.

- creates a ready pool of prospects for full financial planning.

- creates a future book of business for junior brokers.

- builds more relationships for the bank.

I understand the transactional stuff is not the fun part. We feel less valuable to those clients, and they are frankly not as profitable long-term. Further, there is a push by every bank for deeper relationships, more insurance business, more managed money, and less transactional work.

There will be a time to be selective, but the way huge producers got to where they are was by bringing on clients—a lot of them—and then turning the good ones into comprehensive financial planning clients. They cut off portions of their book to junior advisors along the way, or at a minimum of having support staff to handle service.

It will later be your challenge to look for ways to shift the client from the transactional mindset to a relationship mindset.

Note that this is a challenge if you will be doing all of the service work on your own. It's hard to manage service for potentially over a thousand households without a sales assistant or junior advisor. If you don't have help now, when you follow this plan, you'll get to production levels that will justify acquiring help. If the bank has a problem with that, have a real conversation about the service levels the bank would like you to have with their clients, and your ability to continue to produce revenue. Gently remind them that while you manage, for example, $50 million, they may have branches that have the same assets with five or six employees.

First and always: you need a lot of prospects. Whatever avenue you take for prospecting (and this book presents a good number), you have to do it well and you have to do it consistently. You want to earn, at a minimum, *one new prospect per day*. If your opportunity is ample and your execution is even average, you should make a sale of some sort four out of five days.

The closing ratio in the bank is usually not a big issue when incorporating branding, going through the sales cycle thoughtfully, and recommending an investment that matches the need. If you get one new prospect per day, you should be able to close at least four of them per week.

At a minimum, focus on what I call "assets under administration"—meaning money you have made a recommendation on even if it is a bank product (CD, money market, savings, etc.) or at another institution. We are all familiar with the traditional assets under management, or AUM. That is *investment* money that you manage, nothing new there. But be purposeful about your assets under administration. This is money that you helped someone with. You know exactly where it is, how much it is earning, and when it is liquid. You haven't necessarily been paid on it, but you will have another opportunity in the future. Not only should you be tracking that in your contact management system (remember the CRM software for tracking all your prospect and client interactions?) for follow-up, but you should also specify to the client that when they are ready to do something else with that money, to give you a call. And then set a reminder to call them.

I have an advisor friend who estimates his AUM at about $250 million but has an additional $250 million in AUA, or assets under administration. It is just a matter of time before a good portion of it lands in his AUM.

The Appointment

Every single word with a prospect should be scripted. This harkens back to the need for preparation and the need to understand your product menu in fine detail (refer to Chapter 7 on the product menu). That knowledge slides easily into a script. It should sound natural and conversational! But you should know exactly what you are going to say, and it should be practiced.

The professionals make it sound easy because they have done it thousands of times. They can focus less on what they are saying and more on how they say it. They can handle remarks or questions from their clients during their presentation without losing their train of thought.

You have to know your script in order to do that. If there is hesitancy in your process, it comes across as nervousness, lack of knowledge, or inexperience—and any of those perceptions destroys trust . . . often before you've even started to build a relationship.

Small Talk

It starts here and it seems simple, but I have both hired and trained advisors who do this poorly. The goal of small talk is to establish common ground. You can talk about the weather, or who you think will do well in March Madness, or whether they are going to dive into the shopping crowds on Black Friday. But it should go beyond that to create a shared connection. People like people similar to themselves, so you have to find something in common so that in their head, you seem like them.

This is the basis for trust. This is how you open them to the possibility of liking you.

Some examples of small talk: you both went to the same high school. You both drive pickup trucks. You both like hamburgers. You both have two daughters.

Just find some little thing you share in common.

It doesn't hurt to even say, "You're like me, we both think we need four-wheel drives." Or, "We both really love those Vikings!" Or, "Wow, we may have more in common than we knew." Solidify in their subconscious that you are the same as each other. It's human nature to feel more comfortable around "sameness" than around "differentness."

Transition

The transition in your script is key because it sets the stage and can be a quick turn-off if done poorly. Here are the two scenarios you will see most often:

1. If the client happens to come in specifically and proactively looking for financial advice but has not stated which "piece of money" or what goal he wants to discuss, you can simply transition from small talk with "What can I do to help you today?" This is how a doctor sets the stage in a consultative, helpful way.

2. But what if the client already stated the primary reason he has for coming in last week when he made the appointment with you? Or what if you've already made a statement about why you have invited him in, because it was you who proactively set it as the reason for the appointment? Your transition or segue into the business part of your meeting must—for credibility and trust-building—*refer to the stated reason*. This proves that you were listening and taking notes to remember! It is that reason that sets the stage for your discussions.

The reality is that you should be going after many of your appointments very proactively—making list calls, calling after a seminar, calling from a branch referral, etc. If you make a call off a CD maturity list to make your appointments with clients, and they come in to see you and you open with "What can I do for you today?" the smart answer for them would be "I don't know, you called me." Trust and credibility are lost. Instead, you ask a specific transitional question like, "What are your thoughts about that CD that's coming due?"

Or simply start with this: "The reason I called you in today is because I was concerned about this account (*the CD, the money market, or point to a bank account on an account list if you have one*), because a lot of our clients have opted to do something better."

By saying "a lot of clients," you emphasize the bank relationship (which you are leveraging) and the herd mentality (they will not want to get left out of what "everyone" is doing). The word "better" is good to stir up curiosity and the thought that they're not doing as well as they could be.

Front Talk

Somewhere between the small talk transition and profiling, you need to talk about yourself professionally. When you establish why they are with you in this appointment, this is where you insert your brand and tell them about yourself.

Be sure to include your affiliation with the bank. Because at this moment, you are fully leveraging the client's relationship with the bank, the bank's brand, and the trust the client has in the bank. Possible things to say:

"I have worked at the bank for X years."

"The reason I work in the bank is because it allows me more time to work with clients and get to know people in the community."

"I tend to be fairly conservative when working with clients, so the bank is a good fit for me."

"I like working in the bank because I like being part of a team."

Tighten up that branding statement!

Key Focus: One Account or Piece of Money

The appointment should be earmarked for one discussion, or about one piece of money-in-motion, or about one financial goal the client has brought to you for discussion. This makes the process simple and won't feel overwhelming to your client. The goal is to show value, help them solve a problem, and to some degree, give them what they want. (Remember the old saying: "Sell them what they want and *then* sell them what they need.")

People Like to Talk About Themselves

And this moves you from your transition phase to your profiling phase of the conversation. And to do that, you need to "ask a few questions to see where we are at." That is your shift into profiling. Or it might sound like this. "Let me ask a few questions, so I can see what would be better for you in your current situation." And profiling begins.

Goals for Profiling

I have long said, "Anything you say can and will be used against you." I don't really mean that in a court-of-law sense, of course. In profiling, we want to get ahead of client objections. They tell you their situation and what the money is for; you are going to match the appropriate recommendation based on their need.

If you are truly making a good recommendation based on their situation, there should be no *real* objections. (We will discuss objections in Chapter 10, but here's a preview: the primary objections to collect substantial information about are liquidity, safety, and rate.)

If they say they are going to use the money to buy a boat in two years, you tell them that the bank is running a special on a two-year CD. Then, if they come back and say, "Well, I might need it before then," you go back to profiling and re-address the answers they gave you to clarify the goals. Doing this allows you to then make another recommendation.

In the appointment's profiling phase, you do not really need to use a profiling form unless your firm requires it. Although some advisors ask a client or prospect to complete an information sheet before the initial appointment, consider it a bold move— even if every doctor in America does it! If you are newer in the business, however, I think it's better to use a simple form than to try to wing it. Being able to profile conversationally is a practiced skill. Seasoned professionals make it look easy, but it does take practice. Most advisors will use some kind of file-sized notepad to take notes from the conversation. I am not a fan of taking notes on a computer as it can be distracting to the conversation.

Additional profiling focus is on two critical sets of information. Be sure to capture: 1) answers to suitability questions you will need in order to fill out a new account application, and 2) questions, data, information, or specific fields you will want to fill in on your contact management system.

One of the common challenges we face is that clients are put off by profiling questions. They don't get any such questions when they open a CD or checking account (aka those transactional banking encounters).

When you meet resistance, confidently state, "This is how I get to know what will be best for you. What is best for you may not have been best for the client I met with yesterday. And I don't want anything we do today to conflict with anything else you have."

If you aren't confident with your answer to this, next time you visit a doctor and she asks what medications you are currently taking, ask her why she needs to know that. Pay attention to how she answers and mimic that tone!

Another Word on Transactional Business

Many will disagree with me about starting a relationship with a transactional sale. And there is certainly a time and place to not do it. When the client comes in seeking financial *advice*—for instance, saying something like, "I really feel like all of my accounts and investments are too scattered . . . " you can jump right into a more in-depth financial planning process.

Other times, you'll recognize that a prospect's situation is so complex or so problematic that you would be doing a disservice to them by not taking a step back and slowing the process down.

Just remember what one of my own early mentors told me: "Until they sign their name on your forms, they are no more your client than they are anyone else's." The transactional sale can be the client's first step of commitment toward accepting you as their primary financial advisor and having you collect all of their assets.

CHAPTER 9

THE PRODUCT PRESENTATION AND THE RISK CONTINUUM

In order to know how to present your products, we need to back-track just a bit. You have to determine whether you have an *investor* or a *saver* in front of you. (If you have been in the business for a while, you already know what I mean.) There are different ways to sell to each one respectively.

One of the biggest mistakes I see advisors make is when they treat savers like investors and vice versa. It is sometimes challenging to make the distinction based on a short conversation, but get it wrong, and all that does is scare them both away.

Investors may have one or more financial advisors. They will pay a fee when they see value. They understand the risk-and-return correlation better than most people. They see value in a professional opinion. Investors generally have more understand-ing and trust in "the system"—insurance companies, money managers, etc. They may be coming in for an appointment based on a solicitation or proactively inquiring for help, better rates, or investment advice. The investor is potentially more investment-savvy than the saver.

Savers are often risk- and fee-averse. They usually do not have a primary financial advisor. They may not really know what such a professional can do for them. They tend to be distrustful of advice and see it all as coming from "salespeople," and they certainly hate to be sold to! These will usually be people that you have called in to meet with you.

Again, you have to educate these two groups from a different angle. They should be presented to and closed in different ways. And that means you need to know which one is which!

Let's have a closer look at each one respectively.

Selling to Investors

Investors are open to a more traditional financial planning process—they may be more willing to disclose assets and consolidate accounts. They will utilize technology more readily, and they prefer a more direct approach.

If they trust you—and they must trust you because they are more savvy consumers—they expect fact-based, professional opinions based on what is best for them. Like most people, investors make emotional decisions when buying investments and then look to support or justify that decision with logic.

Ask them questions like these:

"What is your favorite investment that you have owned?"

"Are there any investments that you have owned that you did not like?"

"Describe your ideal investment."

These questions allow them to draw on their experience to give you more information.

It is very helpful for investors to see a process and then see your recommendation. It may be a full financial plan or a calculator—like a life insurance calculator or a retirement income gap calculation. These things solidify the logic (the head), which satisfies the emotions (the gut), and when you check those two boxes, there is a very good chance the investor will do business with you.

Simply put, this is a traditional financial advisor-client relationship that you may have gained some experience with at other firms before you came to work in the bank. You will converse with the investor at the bank much like how you would have with a client before you joined the bank.

Selling to Savers

Savers have more fears and are, in fact, quite risk-averse. They are sometimes not very investment-savvy. They will say things to express these attitudes, such as, "I don't want to make more money because it will increase my taxes." They are wary of financial advisors. You can already hear the words in their head: *All of you are just salespeople and want me to pay you that commission!*

Savers also assume they don't need your help, or they assume they don't have enough money to even need you. They believe that your fees are high, and your products are far too long-term for comfort, and that whatever you recommend is going to be risky. Their biggest fear? That they won't understand what you are talking about.

Savers may have bought an investment here or there, but probably don't have a trusted primary financial advisor. Yet these are the individuals who will buy a (often inappropriate for them) mutual fund with their newly-minted financial advisor brother-in-law George out of pure family loyalty. What's worse, it was probably the asset class "du jour" and then went down, which further entrenched them in their "saver" ways. Savers' biggest distinction is that risk is their primary driver in selecting an investment. For this reason, we must often consider risk and volatility above all—even above financial goals.

These attributes and beliefs have led some of the savers you'll meet to make some poor financial decisions on their part in the past, but their mistakes usually erred on the side of conservative. Pay special attention to these people. Because while they can be frustrating, they can provide huge opportunities for us in the bank setting. I have met some advisors who have said they just aren't going to deal with these types of people anymore, but in my opinion, there are too many of them with too much money, opportunity, and need for us to ignore.

Selling Along the Risk Continuum

Once when I was traveling through Iowa, calling on advisors, I met with an advisor whom I knew socially. I didn't know much about his business, however. I knew he was a big producer, and I knew he was very successful based on the size of his business in the tiny midwestern town he was located in. He was generating revenue numbers you would expect from a Downtown Chicago private wealth advisor, and he was only in his early thirties at the time.

I asked him how he ran such a great business. We talked a lot about prospecting, building relationships with the staff, etc., and

I then asked him what he does in front of clients. What I then witnessed was the most talented individual I have ever met at communicating and putting things into words that *anyone* can understand.

It was so brilliant that I quickly planned another trip through Iowa. Only this time, I brought a video camera and set it up in the corner of his office and said, "Do that again." I studied that video in-depth and went on to train many, many advisors using this strategy. I call it "Selling Along the Risk Continuum."

This strategy is absolutely the best way to sell to savers. And there is nothing wrong with using it for investors, too.

The heart of it—as that Iowa advisor tells it—is that "people can tell when you are doing something *with* them versus when you are doing something *to* them."

Learning the Risk Continuum Approach

Be sure that you include this statement in your front talk:

"Part of my job is to help people make decisions."

With your prospect or client, use a whiteboard on your office wall if possible. Or pull out a legal pad they can see, so they can follow along with you. You are going to tell your prospect, "Let's talk about all the options out there, and together we will make a decision."

Across your board or paper, write out all the options you offer—going *from most conservative to most aggressive.* The concept of the continuum is to move gradually and logically from one (low) level of risk and return to the next (higher) level of risk, which leads to the next, and so on.

Draw a line from the lower left to the upper right, and then write down the product categories going up the line, starting with the very conservative moving up to the most aggressive solutions or products. This creates a visual, so the client can see and feel the increase in both risk and potential return.

Let me reiterate: this point in the presentation is where you will utilize your product menu. Not the individual product companies, but the product *categories* that you offer. You are going to break it down into two possible routes/categories based on your profiling:

1. Accumulation (or wealth building)

2. Income (or protection of current wealth with a way to take monthly, quarterly, or annual money out of it for your costs of living)

You want to emphasize that this will demystify the investment world—and this is basically everything that is out there, apart from slight product variations. The key to this is that you want the client to know *you have all the options.* Communicate that they will not have to go across the street to another institution and get some other, different magical option that you don't have. Because you "have it all," there is no reason they shouldn't just work with you, especially when you make this process so easy.

If you find out from profiling that the client is going to take income off of the account, your risk continuum might look something like this, from most to least conservative:

1. Immediate annuity (most conservative)

2. GLWB rider on an annuity (indexed or variable)

3. Fixed annuity

4. CD (seems more conservative but actually more aggressive as it's a bet on shorter-term rates)

5. Systematic withdrawals from an indexed annuity

6. Systematic withdrawals from mutual funds

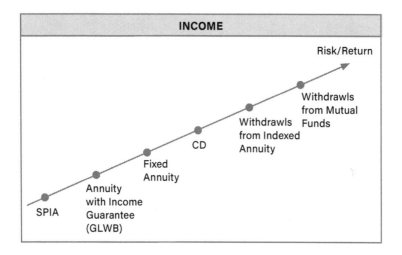

If you find this client is all about the accumulation of money or wealth-building, you will walk through the categories of options that you offer. This may look like:

1. CD

2. Fixed annuity

3. Indexed annuity

4. Registered indexed annuity

5. Variable annuity

6. Mutual funds (if you use managed money, UITs, or REITs, I would lump them together right here for the sake of simplicity, and then go further into them during specific product recommendations)

7. Individual stocks (immediately note that you don't recommend individual stocks, and if they think that is the way they want to go, say they are better off opening an online brokerage account, then immediately cross that off as an option—this at least shows that you acknowledge it as an option)

Another useful step is to draw a dotted line between investments where loss of principal becomes a possibility. That's an easy-to-understand differentiator, and it also gets you in front of any future objections related to risk. We've all had clients that balk at a fixed annuity because they've heard that you can lose money in an annuity. If you get to a specific product recommendation for a fixed annuity, you can refer back to this process you just went through and remind them that fixed annuities were to the left of the line that signified risk of principal, but that there are other annuities to the right of the line that did involve risk.

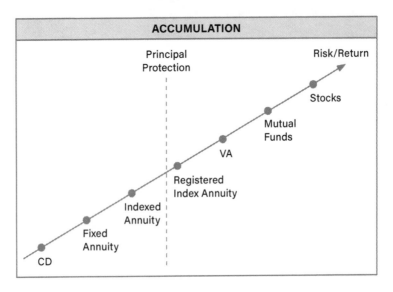

The next steps of the process are to eliminate options that don't make sense but without giving product details. There is no point in giving much detail and confusing them when a product is definitely not a good option. You want to say, "Because you told me X, then Y and Z investments don't make sense. So we won't discuss those." And then immediately mark them off your list.

For example, "You told me this IRA really needs to grow and that you're really hoping to do a lot better than CD rates. So we won't talk about CDs or fixed annuities." And then mark those two options off your list.

By *eliminating options*, you will avoid product overload if trying to explain differentiators and details of multiple products. Prospects can understand the differentiators of two or three options, but not five or six of them.

Once you have it narrowed down to a couple of options (hopefully two but possibly three), you give the thirty-second overview of each in order to garner interest to know where to focus further. It's a decision tree, a way to make a decision. With each step you take, you give slightly more information in order to differentiate—thus further helping them make the decision.

Rates and Returns

Part of what the prospect or client may want to know—and what may help them make a decision—is rates of return.

I know what their first question will be: "What's the rate?"

There is nothing wrong with giving them ballpark returns. (At some point, you do need to talk about expectations of returns.) If you can keep them more focused on the features of the product that are a real fit for them, you'll do better in the end.

By using the process of elimination, you want to either mark things off your whiteboard or legal pad list, or leave them for more explanation later. If you have ever played the kids' game Hotter and Colder, it's a lot like that—sometimes you're talking through the information you collected in profiling. You are creating a decision tree for the client.

Here are two great ways to explain those shortlisted products:

1. Use a T-chart of pros and cons. Be very honest and direct. For example, on a fixed annuity:

   Pros might be ...
   - locks in a rate that won't drop
   - tax deferral
   - keeps money safe

   Cons might be ...
   - locks most money up for five years
   - rate is only slightly better than CDs

   Have your T-chart memorized for every single option you offer, but still write it out for the prospect.

2. Use happy faces and sad faces. Everyone can understand that you want to make sure they are happy no matter what happens, depending on the possibilities of the account. Through your presentation, as you talk about market events and changes to the account, ask them, "Would you be happy or upset if this happened?" If they say happy, draw a happy face to reinforce to them that it might be a good option. But if they have a sad face on the board or page, you both need to know what that means to them or how it will affect them.

   If you are discussing mutual funds and you explain that there will be a time that they get a statement that the account value is less than they started with, not many will say they will be happy. But still talk through what a sad face means to them and actually draw a sad face. Ask if, at this point, they would panic or hold on. Maybe you can change a sad face to a happy face. It's just a decision tree. It helps them pick what's right for them.

Now take a picture of your whiteboard or tear out the paper you have been using and put it in their file. If they come back to you six months later and say they can't handle volatility, you can refer back to the notes and say something like, "Remember when we talked about _____?"

Or if they chose something with a set interest rate, but the equity markets have gone up substantially and they are now unhappy, putting that paper back in front of them can help them remember why they made that decision. And then ask them probing questions to find out what's changed. (It can even be a change of heart with regard to risk tolerance.)

Case Study

Say that you are meeting with a client. While profiling, you find that you're actually discussing money that they don't plan on spending any time soon. They don't need income from it but do not want to put that principal at risk.

You do your front talk, describing your brand and explaining that you help people make decisions. You write out your risk continuum of product categories based on an accumulation case.

Maybe you draw a dotted line down the middle to intersect with your risk continuum and title it "principal protection." Then, you point out that everything to the right of that dotted line carries some kind of risk to the principal. You put a line through everything to the right of that line, saying, "You told me you do not want any risk to your principal with this piece of money, so none of these would be appropriate."

You might suggest then that a CD is not a valid option at this time either because the client has no liquidity concerns and no stated need for cash in the near term. Thus, there is no reason to stay so short term. Put a line through CDs as an option.

This will narrow their options down to a few things on your product shelf that are slightly more aggressive than a CD, but won't put their principal at risk. Based on your product menu, this will give them two or three things that you can now discuss more with them. Your client has gained a general understanding of how these products fit into the investment world, so you can go the next level deeper on differentiators.

Your conversation is essentially a process of elimination, but one you're doing *together.* Two things to remember:

1. You are doing it *with* them and not *to* them.

2. Sometimes you have to sell them what they *want* before you can sell them what they *need.*

Annual Reviews

Another tip with using this risk continuum approach to help a prospect or client make the best decision is to go through the exact same process of presenting "all the investment possibilities" in your annual review appointments. (You *are* making those appointments, right?)

To open that review, you say, "Let's remember how we got here." It's a sort of sum-up of what you've both said together, which is, "You told me A, so we eliminated B. Then you told me X, so we eliminated Y and Z. You said C, and so we kept this on the shortlist..." and so on. Or, "This is how we landed on this option, and here's what we did with your money. Remember? But does it still make sense for you at this time?"

Bring up the goals they shared with you, so that they know you were listening.

The key question to have your client answer is this: "Does this money still belong here?" The market may be down, or they may have a time commitment based on what they chose, but you have an obligation to clearly understand if their risk tolerance has changed.

Talk about performance and how it more than likely fits the possible expectations you set with them, and again review possible expectations for the next year. This also sets the stage for further profiling and uncovering of more assets.

As you again lay out the risk continuum and review how their decision was made, you then insert, "Oh, by the way, do you have other CDs? Is there anything we should note for you under fixed annuities? What about indexed annuities? Do you own any of those?" Gather those assets, too.

Why? For three reasons:

1. You now have more of their trust.

2. They understand better how you work with them.

3. They understand—and hopefully appreciate—your low-pressure, consultative decision-making approach and are happy to let you do more of it on other financial items relevant to them.

Category vs. Company

You will notice that we have not yet mentioned specific products in any way. We have not said, "I know you own X Brand Name Mutual Fund, but you would be better off in Y Brand Name Mutual Fund," and from there gone into battle over expense ratios, standard deviations, and upside capture ratios. Not at all! At this point, you are making product decisions based on the right product *category* for them, *not the right company*.

Once the product category has been chosen, go to your product shelf and make a decision based on what is on your shelf. To the client, you'd say, "It sounds like you should be in a mutual fund. When I use mutual funds with my clients, this is the great company we use," and you explain what is on your shelf. This eliminates the need for multiple products that don't serve your purposes. I suggest you go with an assumptive close (you assume they're going to approve of your recommendation) on a specific product, because in adherence with your product menu, you have no intention of going shopping for a different product for the client (except in extreme cases). If they question your company, explain your due diligence process and move on.

Always relate the company's product back to the product category. This is very important because the focus should be on the product *type*, not nuances between one provider versus the other. That due diligence should lie with you, as the advisor, who has the training and experience to discern product differences. Again, this reinforces the value of the product menu—and your advice to the prospect.

Say you have two choices for indexed annuities. Maybe you have one option with a return of premium rider and one without. You would simply say, "When I use indexed annuities with my clients, I use one of two choices, and here's the difference. Which do you prefer?" Or you already know from profiling what they need, so you decide for them: "Based on what you have told me, this one would make sense."

Short-Term and Risk-Averse Savers

Using this method, you will undoubtedly sell a lot of CDs. As you know, I am in favor of not using brokered CDs but prefer to use the bank's CDs—but that is your decision.

Also, these are AUA, Assets Under Administration, and when the CD comes due, you proactively call them (using your CRM software tool to track CD maturities) and bring the client back in to say, "I know we went through this, but to review our options . . . " and go back through the risk continuum with them. That the options haven't changed that much will comfort them. It allows you to take updated notes on any new needs and new goals they've developed since your last meeting and decisions. Further to the point: it allows you to continue to build trust and confidence. Always, always build trust.

Maybe this is when you start asking the questions for deeper profiling, such as, "Do you have any of these annuities, or these mutual funds, or these stocks? Why don't we get together again next week and review your statements to make sure that money is in the right place too?"

They may tell you things they didn't tell you the first time— and they will be comfortable doing so because they know you now, they know your style, and they have greater trust in you.

The key is that every time the CD comes due, you have a valid reason to get together with the individual.

Don't Move Too Fast

If you try to treat a saver like an investor, you will likely lose them. If their money has been in a CD for ten years and it's ear-marked—in their mind—as their safe money, respect that. If you don't, and you tell them they really should put it all in mutual funds, you will likely lose them. You become untrustworthy. You haven't "heard" them. This is one example of how employing the risk continuum process prevents you from making such mistakes!

I often say that you can only take people up one or maybe two steps at a time. If they have CDs, you might get them into a fixed or indexed annuity. If they have an indexed annuity, you might get them to go into mutual funds. But you probably won't get them to go all the way from CD to a mutual fund; that may be too big of a leap for them to make in terms of complexity and risk.

Remember that your job is not to do what is best for the client. Your job is to do what's best for your client *that they will allow you to do for them*. Sometimes that may be what's best for them, and sometimes it may not be, but in the end, it is their money and their decision. Help them make a decision. Help them find the right home for the money.

The risk continuum approach, used with both savers and investors, takes the pressure off of you to recommend the perfect category and product. (And we know there is no such thing.) It also takes the pressure off of you to predict market performance as you are preparing them for possible outcomes. It helps the prospect say to you, "*This* is what I have been looking for." At this point, the prospect is buying and not being sold to. People love to buy, but remember how much they hate to be sold to!

This risk continuum sales approach is so non-threatening that people actually enjoy the process of making sure their money is in the right place and feeling that they are learning more and participating in making those educated decisions. You have become a trusted resource. They will bring you more money to put through the process. They might refer others to you down the road.

The extension of this process is that the bankers will see you suggesting CDs (and other appropriate bank products) to clients, giving them a comfort level about the work you are doing inside their bank and for their clientele.

With the risk continuum process, you are genuinely helping people—educating them, listening to their needs and goals, helping them purchase just what they want or need, as opposed to selling them things. This will help your brand, your circles of relationships, and your referrals.

CHAPTER 10

KNOW THEIR OBJECTIONS BEFORE THEY DO

This wouldn't be a business-building, sales-strategy book without addressing objections. All sales gurus say and teach this: know your clients' objections and work the answer into your upfront presentation. That way, the client won't present the objection at any critical later stage in the process since you've already responded to it.

Here are some core objections that you will encounter every day in bank and credit union settings.

Proper Profiling

As I mentioned, I have long said, "Anything the prospect says during profiling can and will be used against them."

Okay, okay, it's a horrible analogy—it sounds like they're being arrested. But my point is that when a prospect tells us one thing in the profiling process and then changes that detail during the product decision-making process, we have to back-pedal and find out what's really true. We need to go back and get clarification or confirmation.

The importance of proper profiling is to get ahead of the prospect to make sure we are matching the right investment to their set of needs, wants, and goals. If you're facing a rough sea of objections, then you may not be talking about the right product category at all.

Don't mistake objections for unrealistic expectations. I know we all want 10% per year with full liquidity and FDIC/NCUA insurance. Those aren't objections. Those are unicorns and mermaids—things none of us will ever find.

The fact that all prospects hang on to this ideal investment emphasizes the value of selling along the risk continuum, as I laid out in Chapter 9. The risk continuum lays out all possible objections and lets prospects sort out their most important concerns as you move along the continuum. If they like fixed annuities but insist on a six-month term, then a CD might be the best we can do. If they want the unlimited upside potential of mutual funds but aren't comfortable with the possibility of losing money that also comes with owning mutual funds, then a fixed or registered indexed annuity might be the best we can do.

All that said, there are 3.5 objections you will face on a regular basis. (Yes, three and a half—not a typo!) There are a handful of others that you may have heard about while at other firms, such as, "I already have an advisor" and "I do all my own investing." Those are normal objections that all advisors face outside of the bank. You need to be ready to overcome those as well, but for now, let's focus on the ones you see the most.

The 3.5 objections we face are:

0.5 Fees

1. Rate

2. Liquidity

3. Safety

Fees

I only count an objection to fees as a half-objection because I don't think it's a real one. Unless the client walked to the bank, they saw value in paying for something that provides a service. They paid for the car and the gas for the car because they saw value and benefits in that cost when compared to walking to the bank.

If someone is objecting to the fee, they simply don't see value in what you are suggesting. In the face of *perceived value*, cost is rarely an objection. There's always a cheaper way to go. That makes one of your jobs presenting the value of the product and your assistance to them, so that the fee seems a minimal issue or none at all.

There's a reason people buy a top-of-the-line Mercedes when they can reach the same destinations in a mid-range Honda. Re-explain the value they are getting (and have your value statement refined in advance—preparation!) and if they still have a problem, say, "I didn't realize that cost was your biggest driver in choosing an investment, so let me show you what we can do that has no fees." Be humble; do not display any sarcastic tone! Be obliging. Be literal. Show them. When appropriate, demonstrate how the no-fee option does not suit their requirements. Again reinforce that choosing an investment purely based on the fee is the tail wagging the dog. Explain that any cost or fee may pay off in terms of growth potential, guaranteed income, tax advantage, etc. And then do the best you can for them based on *what they will allow you to do* for them.

Fees can be a real sticking point for clients, so you must learn a neutral, humble approach to educating them. I have often said that bank clients would prefer a CD paying 1% versus a CD paying 4% with a 1% fee. If they tell you that they follow one of the TV talking heads who promotes never paying a fee, the best way to overcome that is to explain that those people do great work on debt counseling. (As in, "Should I pay my mortgage down first or start by paying off my student loan?") They are fine for early savers—as in, "Start an emergency fund, next put $50 per month into a mutual fund"—but the more positive your net worth, the less value they add.

Your script, in this case, might be this:

"Mr. Brown, in your situation, very little of what they talk about on TV is relevant. For you, we need to consider _____ *(product allocation, asset allocation, tax minimization strategies, a retirement income plan, potential maximization of social security, estate planning)."*

Rate

An objection to the rate, although I count it as a full objection, is more a set of unrealistic expectations.

This objection may be based on having had CDs pay double-digit returns many years ago, or hearing from friends or family about the fantastic returns they received on the one stock they picked that actually made money, or possibly just an idea of what they *want to make*, which may not be rooted in reality at all.

You want to be sure you are giving them clear and realistic expectations and never exaggerating possible returns. You want to have future conversations answering, "Are we on track?" based on those *estimated* returns. (Not *promised*. You never can, and so never should, make promises.)

I will caution you, though. One thing that savers have a hard time understanding is your answer to the question "What is the rate?" If you are talking about a CD or a fixed annuity, a rate is easy to quote. If you are talking about an indexed annuity or a mutual fund, it's not as easy. Investors get it; savers do not. The concept that you cannot just quote a rate but only a dividend *yield* is suspicious and uncomfortable to them.

You must explain, "We won't know the total return for the year until the end of the year because we are measuring growth, not just a rate."

This is a simple concept for an advisor, granted. Keep in mind, though, that it is totally foreign to a "saver" bank customer who has been trained to focus on rate. Put yourself in their shoes and explain clearly.

The best way to explain away this rate concern is simply this:

> "Based on your telling me X and Y, this choice of Z will give you the best *chance* at growth. I don't know exactly what the return will be from one year to the next, but this will give you the best chance at capturing growth."

That is immensely powerful language—because it's true. *Read that again* because it came from a very successful advisor.

Here is how that might look to your specific client:

> "Based on your telling me that you are comfortable with taking some risk but don't want to suffer through the full

market downswings, a registered index annuity will give you the best chance at growing your money."

Keep in mind the educational process that the client goes through with selling and explaining across the risk continuum. The puzzle pieces will fit together. For example, they should now understand that if they buy a mutual fund and put their money at risk, with a long-term expectation of averaging between 6% and 10%, then they probably aren't going to get a fixed annuity paying 6%. It just makes sense that it wouldn't be available. But they may still ask for it.

Liquidity

Everyone wants all their money liquid—available as cash at a moment's notice. They don't know why, but they do. We know why and it is this: people in a panic feel more secure with cash in their hands than with that same cash "locked up."

With bank clients, liquidity is a primary concern. There are a few strategies for overcoming this objection, but there is a bigger issue that needs to be addressed first.

Remember that profiling is the key to getting ahead of objections. Ask the client what money they keep liquid in case of emergencies. Prime the pump with hints:

"What liquid money do you have in checking accounts? In money markets? In savings accounts? In short-term CDs under two years?"

Ask the question. And don't let silence compel you to answer for them!

Ask them to imagine the most expensive emergency they can think of, and what it would cost them—then ask them to think of how much cash they'd need to cover it.

Tell them, "When I work with people, I usually recommend X months' worth of living expenses held as cash or as liquid assets. However, for you and your goals, I'm thinking we should play it extra conservative and go with Y *more* months of living expenses in liquid assets." Show them that you are being conservative with them, that you have their best interests at heart.

Explain "liquidity strategies" within investment choices. In other words, tell them which instruments provide liquidity on demand and which ones only after a certain holding time. Explain that a particular annuity may become liquid after the initial term expires. Explain the liquidity of mutual funds or managed accounts (although you have to be careful with this one, because shortening the holding period in their mind also shortens the expectation for how long it should take you to meet long-term average expectations). The goal of your explanations is to ensure they understand that while they may be long-term strategies, liquidity is available.

Here is the issue underlying the above strategies: *your client has rarely or never thought through an emergency financial (aka a liquidity/cash) plan.* If the subject of liquidity seems overwhelming to a particular client, maybe you call a timeout to the meeting and confront it. Essentially, return to the profiling mode and 1) learn more about the client, and 2) educate him further.

Say, "It seems you are very worried about what will happen if there is an emergency, and you need an unusual amount of cash. Why don't we make a plan for which 'buckets' of money we go to first for that cash? That way, you have a plan, you know your strategy, and you know where the ready money is. And I'll also know your strategy. If something happens to one of you (*assuming you are talking to a couple*), you can come to me, and I can help you remember what we'll do. Another benefit to you of doing this with me now is that we have a plan for liquidity with some of your money. Then, with the rest of your money, we can earn some interest. We never really make money on those short-term liquid accounts."

Note that we are no longer focusing on the initial money we were discussing. The appointment has looped back to profiling—specifically, finding out more about how the client thinks about their emergency needs and educating them about solutions. The discussion becomes about liquidity planning or cash flow.

There is, perhaps, no *immediate* gratification or commission for you. But remember that sometimes you have to sell them what they want before you can sell them what they need. What they want is safety and comfort—to know that no matter what the emergency, they will have liquid assets.

This may be the most basic of all financial planning, but this matter of "liquidity for life's surprises" may be something they have never really put clear thought into. They don't do it because they don't know how to do it. Sometimes it scares them to think of a "personal crisis." They have only worked on one financial plan, while you have worked on hundreds. That's value worth repeating! Tell them that!

Safety

The third full objection is about the safety of a client's money.

Many advisors in banks have questioned their own sanity over constantly needing to explain the safety of a fixed or indexed annuity. After all (we ask ourselves), why would a multibillion-dollar insurance company with solid ratings from all rating agencies and a hundred-year history possibly risk it all by not paying you back your $30,000?!

But our clients don't know this. We must educate them.

Many prospects and clients see the financial world as complex. They honestly don't know their "safe money alternatives." That is why we have jobs! Come from the client's perspective and talk about protecting their money with them. Education eases objections.

There are other solutions that provide safety outside CDs. This could include other principal-protected products or the power of diversification through portfolios.

I would suggest three strategies:

1. **Make safety the core reason for any of your recommendations.** If a recommendation is made, "Safety is exactly why we are deciding on this option." You might follow this with "If I thought there was a chance that you would lose your money, I wouldn't be recommending this to you, because you specifically said you didn't want to put your money at risk."

2. **Refer to the due diligence process of your broker-dealer or bank.** If it is an insurance product, you could say something like "We go through a rigorous research process in selecting the insurance companies we work with. We could find you a better rate with a smaller or lower-rated insurance company, but through our research, we have found this company to not only give great rates but to also be very stable financially." Or, if it's an investment product, "There are a lot of good money managers out there. But we have a process to narrow down the list we use to those that have done a very good job over the long run and have provided lower volatility relative to the market while still providing good returns."

3. **Examine what makes them feel unsafe.** There is a chance that it's not the investment they don't trust: *it's you.* If you are

telling them that they won't lose their money, whether it's true or not, they have to believe you. This takes you back to one of our most important rules: clients have to like you and trust you!

A Final Tip

You can answer most objections with "That's exactly why I recommended this."

Bit of a Jedi mind trick, as it initially seems confusing. But if you've truly matched an investment to a prospect's needs, they may just need some clarification or further explanation.

For example, if the client says they do not want any market risk and you propose a fixed annuity, they may say, "But I don't want to lose my money." (As they often say.)

Your response? "That's exactly why I recommended a fixed annuity."

Anecdotally, this objection of safety is not one that is hard to overcome when we are working with a referral from another client. That's because the first client has already vouched for you with the second one; the latter comes to you possessing a great deal of implicit trust. That proves this is a trust issue, not really a question of whether XYZ insurance or investment company is a company they can depend on. Build that same level of trust with any prospect in the time leading up to this point of the appointment, and they won't question you.

If you're constantly getting caught up in client objections, it's time to re-evaluate the process that leads up to that point. Review the objections you have heard from all clients in the past and write them down—along with your approach to respond to them. Prepare to address them in your branding, your front talk, and as you present any product.

CHAPTER 11

LEVERAGING THE TRANSACTIONAL CLIENT

Now you know how to open accounts, one after another, and are doing several a week. Your close ratio is off the charts, and you are making a little money. Success leads to more success; people get more comfortable referring to you. You are legitimately busy, not just looking busy!

This is a phase that I see a lot of bank advisors stuck in: they are making enough money but not making a lot of money. They are only growing marginally each year rather than *exponentially*.

The next step is so simple, but it is one of the steps that makes a difference between average and great. There are two reasons people don't do it.

First, some aren't quite sure how to do it. This is easily remedied, and you'll read how here. As I tell advisors, "When you know the 'what,' you can learn the 'how.'"

Second—and the more challenging hurdle for people—is

that if you feel busy, you may not be taking time to thoughtfully plan your business and the tactics that get you growth. You either believe you don't have the time, or you just never give a thought to the need to strategize the achievement of that growth. (More on that in Chapter 12.)

I tell advisors, "Spend 10% of your time working on your business and 90% of time working in your business."

Part of that 10% planning time should be spent on deciding who you should be approaching to be full-fledged financial planning clients. Well, it's the transactional clients!

You helped them with one account, maybe two. Now you need to go back and get all their money. Transition them: you want to be doing their insurance planning, retirement income planning, social security planning, wealth transfer—and all the rest, whatever "the rest" means for the client. It may include financial planning software and it may not, depending on what is best for the client and how you run your business. It may even be a further series of transactions.

Leverage transactional clients. To leverage:

- Step #1 is getting a steady flow of *bank* prospects.

- Step #2 is to make them *your* clients through a transaction.

- Step #3 is to become their *primary* financial advisor. They return to you with all their new needs and take your periodic calls and appointments.

This is the path for all those transactional relationships, whether new ones going forward or those in your book of business right now. They bought based on the assumption that you were helping them perhaps with a piece of money. Now it's time for you to actually show them how you can help them holistically as their financial advisor.

Let's break your new clients into three tiers:

- **Tier A**—You see real opportunity in this client through their level of assets, attitude, and need for help. If we had to quantify assets (always dependent on your market, socioeconomic surroundings, etc.), maybe it's $500,000 or $750,000 or more in investible assets. Brokerage firms tend to say $1M to $3M+ is their target market. Realistically, in banks and credit unions, we serve more of a middle market of $250,000–$1M in assets. Several of the top producers I have worked with have never had a million-dollar rollover.

- **Tier B**—Maybe this client has a need but minimal assets to work with. Perhaps they do not see a significant benefit to working with an advisor. Quantified, he has maybe $250,000 to $750,000 in assets.

- **Tier C**—This client does not have a lot of assets. They might be a very skeptical buyer, overly fee-averse. They hold little potential to develop future significant assets.

The "Remiss" Conversation

This specific conversational approach helps shift the transactional client into a "planning" client. The setting varies according to tier:

- **Tier A**—Take them to lunch. I know it is not the norm for bank advisors to take clients to lunch, but do it and pay out of your pocket. If adding $750,000 or a million dollars to your AUM is not worth $20 for lunch, you need to examine your compensation plan. It shouldn't be an extravagant lunch, but it shouldn't be a sub sandwich—something in-between.

- **Tier B**—Call them into the office for a meeting. This can be initiated at the time of a review of their first monthly or quarterly statement or a policy delivery, or to help them get set up on a website to view accounts.

- **Tier C**—You probably won't be having this conversation with Tier C clients. If you know there are minimal assets, minimal financial planning can take place; it's not a complex situation. This said, be aware that life happens, and clients can move overnight—up or down—from one tier to another!

This "remiss" conversation is one you must have in person. It goes like this:

"Mr. Brown, I appreciate the opportunity to help you on the _____ (*IRA, CD, or whatever piece of money you discussed to make them clients*). I think it's going to do well for you. Listen, I've been thinking a lot about you and your situation. You remind me of many clients I do a lot more for than just helping with one recommendation. I feel I have been remiss in fully explaining how I can be of service. For example . . . "

At this point, you should know enough about them to know why you would be a good advisor for them. Maybe you know they are nearing retirement and will need a retirement income plan. Maybe they're getting close to making an election on when to draw Social Security. Maybe you have worked with several people who work for the same employer, and you understand that company's pension plan very well. All of these situations open the door for you. If nothing else, provide a sample written financial plan, although maybe don't suggest diving into the entire plan. Point out sections that might specifically help their needs or concerns.

This conversation is never about selling a product or gathering assets—not yet. It's all about selling yourself and building a relationship. The goal is to walk out of the meeting with someone who likes you and trusts you, and who is willing to give you a shot at being their new primary financial advisor. You need to have a specific action plan for the next steps. Now you have an ideal client that will bring assets and hopefully provide referrals to more people just like themselves.

If you bring on three clients in a week, I would guess you'll have an even distribution. That is, you'll have one Tier A, one Tier B, and one Tier C. That should provide at least one client who understands and responds favorably to your "remiss" conversation. If you close three new transactions and bring on one full financial planning client per week, you will be very successful.

It's that easy. It's so easy that you may not believe me. But I've seen it work time and again for advisors across the country and across the spectrum of banks and credit unions. Thoughtfully planning out who you will approach is important, but it doesn't happen until you do it. Like anything else, the second time will go better than the first time, and the third time better than the second.

People love potential. They love to feel valued. Tell them you want to help. Tell them you are the most qualified for the job. And then tell them the next steps. This will lead your business from experiencing marginal annual growth to exponential growth.

Part Three

RUNNING YOUR BUSINESS

You make one sale. And then another. And another. Pretty soon, you're busy all day—or at least as busy as you want to be. So busy that the business seems to be running itself, which can make you feel very successful. The downside is that without preparation and thoughtful planning, you will not get to a million dollars in gross revenue, much less $2M or $3M.

Planning your day is easy. If it's not, I will tell you how top producers do it: they only go to one branch per day. They stack their appointments from the end of the day backward—setting their 4 p.m., then their 3 p.m., then their 2 p.m.—or whatever slots they use. This ensures they are busy until the bell and cuts out annoying gaps of time between appointments. And they all do use appointment slots like doctors. They have a set number of appointment times available every day, and they are pre-set times.

For example, if they have five appointments available per day, they may have a 9 a.m., a 10 a.m., a 1 p.m., a 2 p.m. and a 4 p.m. blocked out. They leave longer appointment times open for first appointments when possible. And they leave time at the end of the day for planning for the next day.

Most of you probably do that daily planning—or could start today. But planning for the next six months, twelve months, or three years is more challenging.

Ironically, corporate American is widely guilty of promoting the "meeting culture." What kind of meetings do we assume those in the ivory tower spend their day in? Meetings with a lot of time *talking about* doing work, of course . . . but not actually *doing work*.

Believe it or not, you should be doing a little bit of that. Talk about what you are going to do. You should be spending

5%–10% of your time *on* your business and the rest of your time *in* your business.

Being in your business means doing the work: prospecting, doing the client-related work such as referral training, setting appointments, preparing presentations, having prospect and client meetings, and managing paperwork. There are other "in-the-business" tasks and activities, but we can agree those are the big ones.

Working *on* the business? This is akin to greasing the moving parts of a machine. You should have regular time every month, if not every week, where you are meeting with the most important people to your business, the ones who make things go smoothly and grow. I am not talking about the regularly scheduled sales pipeline review with your manager, although this can be important. (Your sales manager should be an important person to your team.) But you should have regular pre-set time with every important person on your team: licensed bankers, associate/junior brokers, sales assistants, branch managers, the marketing department, senior bank management, wholesalers, etc. You don't need to meet with them all weekly or even monthly in some cases, but there should be a regular routine. And you should talk *about* the business with them.

Many advisors say they are far too busy to devote that much time to planning or the "on-the-business" side of things. On Monday at 8 a.m. they hop on the treadmill, and they hop off on Friday afternoon at 3 p.m.. That is exactly the issue. It's common sense, but poorly executed: if you take the time away from the treadmill to be more thoughtful about your business, then you don't have to feel like your week is a treadmill—or at least it won't feel like the treadmill is set just slightly too fast.

How are you going to find the prospects? How will you make them clients? How will you maintain them year after year? And how do you put all those greased moving parts together to make for a real, cohesive, growing business?

The chapters in this section will explore some topics that need to be addressed in order for you to say you are running a successful practice. While certainly not inclusive, this is a sampling of topics that have come up consistently over the years in my conversations with top producers. Then, when you're done reading, go set regular meetings with all the stakeholders and business partners in your business!

CHAPTER 12

EVERY BUSINESS NEEDS A PLAN

Don't skip this chapter. And stop rolling your eyes! You need to map out a business plan so that you know where you are going, and if and when you have arrived there. As they say, a goal without a plan is just a dream.

A startup business selling products or services will find out if they have a successful concept only by writing a business plan and testing assumptions. That need to plan exists whether someone is a professional chiropractor, a dentist, a CPA, an attorney—or a financial advisor, like you.

Just because you are in a bank or credit union setting doesn't get you off the hook. Don't treat your activity like a salaried job. Treat it like a business. Set goals and devise a plan to reach them.

I am convinced one reason that advisors don't treat their activity like a business because there is no initial investment on their part. What if the bank told you that you had to write them a check for $100,000 to do your job? Would you pay that much to launch your financial services business within their walls?

Now, we all know that business is numbers. So imagine spending the same $100,000 to own and launch a hamburger franchise. Some of the first numbers you crunch include how much the rent is, how many staff you need and at what rate of pay, your margin on every hamburger, and how many hamburgers you need to sell every month to cover costs. Some of the operational issues you must decide on include how you are going to promote the business in the marketplace and ensure repeat and referral business by customers you've gained. This is typical in any business, and our business is not really that different, is it? Yet so many advisors that I talk to have this attitude: "I'll see where I end up for the month."

Write It Down

Don't underestimate the value and power of 1) thinking through all the moving parts—people, activities, etc., 2) thinking about the goals you want to achieve, and 3) having it all written down to keep you focused. Don't write it nonchalantly just because your sales manager requires it.

I polled top producers on the form their plans have taken, and it varied widely—but it was always *written*. Some showed me spreadsheets that were interactive; some showed me twenty-page written plans that were so detailed that they planned for each lunch hour and what time they would leave the office on Fridays. Just make sure it's in a form that you can review with your team and other impactful partners. There is no right or wrong, but you simply cannot write clearly what you have not thought through. Just make sure it communicates clearly.

Writing a business or marketing plan requires you to first think about the various goals associated with your services, your skill set, and your career. Don't believe that you need only one master goal to achieve success. By answering some of the following questions, you are in fact setting a number of goals:

- Your production goal as *gross revenue.*

- How many new clients will you bring on as transactional clients, and how many will become full financial planning clients? (Back out average gross revenue and average ticket size to get a reasonable number of necessary clients. How many leads and prospects must you generate to have that many confirmed clients? It's an equation!)

- What sort of referral goal do you set as the outcome of the training? What is your referral training plan for the bank personnel in the various branches you serve that helps them achieve their goal?

- How many other business-building events will you hold? What types? How often?

Other Ways to Build a Plan

Think about failures of the past year or two, or things you've said you'd do but regretfully did not. Build the plan by setting higher expectations:

- Think about the moving parts of what you do. Where is there "sand in the motor"?

- Think about what has *not* been going well in recent times that could be improved if you focused on it with the correct knowledge or skills.

- What certifications or other new learning do you wish to undertake?

- Do you need or want a coach/mentor to help move your business to a higher level, or to hold you accountable to the action steps you've written into your new plan?

- What results were you expecting last year? Why do you believe you did or didn't get them? (Review and change expectations—or change what you need to do—for a better outcome this year.)

- What beneficial resources have you hesitated to use? How could you get comfortable with using them?

- What questions or requests have you hesitated to ask that have held you back? How could you get comfortable about asking?

- What new tactics from this book could you be using in the coming weeks and months? (Choose two or three to start.)

How do you achieve your goals? Every plan lists your goals. To achieve goals, you have to do something. The next thing you add to your written plan is the action steps you will take over the next weeks and months to achieve every single goal you have listed.

Action steps are specific and focused. There is no secret that your attention must be on 1) prospecting and 2) running your business. But how you achieve your goals is about taking specific actions day after day with consistency. As all professional athletes know, there are no days off.

For each activity, list the benefit to clients and the bank. List what will be needed from each teammate—i.e., wholesalers, branch managers, your assistant, licensed banker, district bank manager, etc.

For any teammate, be sure they see the benefit of what they provide to you. For instance, if the branch has a sales goal, be sure to show how Activity A will reach X% of the branch goal. Or how one referral training a month will lead to N referrals, which will lead to X% of the team's goal (revenue, assets brought in, etc.).

I know that by now you're saying, "I don't need to do all that." First, I disagree. We all need written, executable goals. Second, even if you don't need it for yourself, you need it for those around you.

The Most Valid Reason to Make a Plan

You are proving to management that you are a real business partner of the bank and a bona fide team member. Your written plan gets others to see you as a business and treat your business with the same seriousness you have about it. Treating your activity or career like a business—and calling it "my business"—is how the top producers make those big results.

Who Sees Your Plan Is a Strategic Decision

Branch managers, senior bank management, your assistant, your team, and wholesalers are the ones who should see (or hear a summary of) your business or marketing plan.

Having a documented plan makes you look methodical. When you cover multiple branches and they just see you come and go from time to time, the plan establishes legitimacy to your business.

This is especially important with senior bank management. Like any senior management, they want their people to be thorough and detailed. When you ask for support and resources, they'll remember your written plan (and perhaps one or two of your business goals), and that your request is purposeful rather than random. They know that when they provide Request #1 *to* you, then it will yield Result #1 *from* you.

The plan is very useful whenever you need new support—lists, referral training opportunities, educational workshop resources, or help from the marketing team. If you need people's time, which costs them money, stress your contribution to their goals as stated in your own plan.

Have both revenue goals and non-revenue goals in your plan. For instance, show the number of loans and bank accounts you will likely refer back to the bank. If you have ever wondered, and advisors do ask me this, "How do I get the bank to let me _____ (*have call lists, do more training, hold a referral contest, etc.*)?" there is your answer—The Business Plan.

Your sales assistant may be included in creating the plan, but be sure to communicate what their expectation is and how they will support every activity. Also, team members like to feel like they are part of something bigger; this can help them feel like mundane tasks are contributing to big goals.

Wholesalers will appreciate that you clearly define what support you need from them and how they will benefit:

- Be reasonable. And don't be surprised if they need to review and come back to you.

- Remember that wholesalers are running a business, too—it's not all steak and golf—and they have to make thoughtful business decisions just as you do. They will respect you more and do more for you when they see that your requests are part of a well-crafted plan.

- If it effectively takes care of X% of their goal that they "don't have to worry about," they'll love that. (Assuming you do your part.)

- Even if the product sales expectation is small for their product, they will respect the transparency and honesty.

- This gives them a training opportunity if there is a hole in the plan where they see some opportunity (either product or practice management).

- This allows them to carve out budget and time—and the earlier in the year you do this, the easier it is for them to plan. For instance, if you know you want to do three business-building events with the wholesaler as the main speaker, book them at the start of the year. You will slide into the wholesaler's travel schedule and budget with little to no challenge!

Your plan should be a living document. Don't just bury it in a drawer. Don't assume you'll never update it or parts of it over the course of the year. When plans change, amend your written plan and again communicate it with those around you. In short, build this plan for you—as your own business GPS—because you need it.

If nothing else, build and document a plan as a marketing tool to get the buy-in that you need from others. Always be selling those around you on the importance of your business and your clients' success.

CHAPTER 13

BUILDING YOUR TEAM

An advisor recently texted me to tell me he had a breakout year, going from $300,000 to $500,000 in gross revenue. He went on to lament that he had worked extraordinarily hard and could not fathom how advisors got to $1,000,000 in gross revenue.

One answer is that they don't do it on their own. You have to spend money to make money, as the cliché goes. It's not *always* true, but luckily for us, the economics work out in our business.

It's fairly easy to cover the costs of having help. Every bank does things a little differently, and how they let advisors structure their team is no exception. It will be a process for you to work through with management, so that they and you are comfortable with the organic development of your team. If you aren't sure how to approach this, go back and re-read Chapter 12 on business plans!

One consistency in my interviews with top-producing advisors is this: *they all have teams and support*. They are the lead advisor, but they surround themselves with reliable, effective, well-trained people.

I know an advisor who has one unlicensed sales assistant, two licensed sales assistants, and two associate financial advisors. He grosses over $3,000,000 per year.

When growing a dedicated team, be sure that team growth leads to revenue growth, too. Then the economics work. The revenue justifies the team—and bank management will not debate the point!

What I Mean by "Your Team"

But let's back up. "Your team" could include frontline staff who give you referrals, bank management, and others—right?

Yes, that is true. And they are true support for your business. But here, I want to talk specifically about:

- LBs or licensed bankers

- Sales assistant(s), licensed and unlicensed

- Junior broker(s)/associate financial advisor(s)

- Sales manager

- Wholesalers

These are the individuals who either have a vested interest in your success, or their job function is specifically to support your success and the success of the team with their particular skills, training, and abilities.

Licensed Bankers

I'll discuss working with licensed bankers in the next chapter in more detail, but when building your team, LBs are fertile recruiting material to move into sales assistant and junior broker functions. If you find LBs who are exceptional at sales, they may step into those roles. They carry instant credibility and likability because they are approachable by the bank staff—they have walked in the banker's shoes.

Sales Assistants, Licensed and Unlicensed (Aka Service Manager)

If you are grossing in the high six figures right now, you may have room for both licensed and unlicensed sales assistants. If you are grossing under $500,000, be aware that you're still better off with a licensed assistant, both for the trading abilities and the bench strength as a potential junior advisor.

Note: An important key to grossing a million dollars is having a sales assistant—I have only met one advisor in twenty years who does it without a sales assistant.

Try this twist: introduce your *sales assistant* to clients as your *service manager*. First, your "assistant" feels the promotion and hopefully lives up to the manager title, however informally you have assigned it. Start training your clients from the first meeting to go to your service manager. I have heard from advisors that they explain to clients and prospects that for "anything investment-related, you should come and talk to me. For anything paper-related, my service manager is the efficient one!"

Not ever calling the person an "assistant" helps achieve this distinction in clients' minds. "Manager" is a much more trusted term by any client.

I have heard from many advisors that they are afraid to delegate. Keep in mind that you simply can't handle every piece of paper and still scale your business to $1,000,000 in gross revenue and beyond. You just cannot do it! You don't speak to your physician to make the next appointment. The dentist with a million-dollar practice doesn't do teeth-cleaning or X-rays but has a dental hygienist do it while he is doing something that only a trained, licensed dentist can do.

Similar to these other well-organized professionals, find out what rote things, what purely administrative things, you do. Determine how to delegate them out so you can focus on the money-making activities.

I have heard many advisors say they don't trust their sales assistant to perform certain tasks. If you don't trust your assistant, then you need to train them! Do that vital work. If not (or if the training doesn't stick), you need to manage them out. While you are probably not their manager according to HR, you can work with whoever is responsible for them.

Two Things Your Sales Assistant Should Not Be Doing

As a rule, money-*administration* matters get delegated to an assistant. Money-*making* and money-*generating* and prospect-*generating* activities are yours—and you never, ever delegate those out.

1. **You should call lists and branch referrals personally.**
   This is one of my biggest frustrations, and you aren't going to change my mind. I often hear from advisors that they don't get enough referrals . . . and then I hear that they don't even make the first call! You aren't so important and so busy that if you get referrals, you can't be calling them yourself. My guess is that you would not do it with client referrals, so why would you do it with branch referrals? No one is going to make that call as well as you do. It's lazy not to pick up

that phone. Those are relationship-building, pipeline-filling opportunities, and that's your responsibility.

2. **Do the staff referral training yourself.** If you have a guest speaker, like a wholesaler, then you have to be present. There is nothing wrong with them hearing it from another voice during a training session as long as you are laying the groundwork. This is crucial time you must use to build a relationship with staff. Having your assistant do referral training actually creates a negative effect. You might be making people come to work early or catching up on their work later because they have to attend a meeting to hear about referrals, and the advisor doesn't even show up to do it themselves?! As one person told me, "That's a deal breaker." In other words, "*No* referrals to the guy who can't even be bothered to show up!"

It sounds absurd, but I hear of it all the time. It is great for your assistant to interact with the staff during the training because that assistant is part of your brand and how you deliver world-class service to their clients. Don't have your assistant conduct training alone.

Junior Brokers and Associate Financial Advisors

Producing gross revenues of a million dollars without a junior broker is challenging but attainable. Producing gross revenue of consistently *more* than a million dollars year after year without a junior broker is challenging, if not impossible.

I suggest not bringing on juniors until you are above $500,000 in gross revenue production. I have met many advisors who are scared to give up geography and accounts. And certainly, if you are grossing $250,000–$500,000, you have the time to prospect and travel.

The fact is this: most advisors producing well over a million dollars in gross revenues have at least one junior broker. Period.

Some banks have them. Some don't. If you can justify a business case for it, most sales managers will find a way to make a junior broker assignment happen. Usually, there is a benefit for compensation to the senior broker, an override or revenue split as an incentive to share their clients—usually cutting off "C" and "D" clients for junior brokers and often sharing some branches or appointments.

Compensation to the junior and senior broker is key because it will drive behavior. When a junior is also compensated for business they refer to the senior, it will be the most valuable referral source you have. They will drive all over town chasing every appointment just as you did in your first few years. Let them find the prospects that are coming in for a 529 plan but have a million dollars. Let the junior uncover that gem in profiling. And even if you aren't actually making the sale, it's passive income for you.

Be sure to set attainable but aggressive goals for them. Don't set a goal of $100,000 in gross revenue the first year. The goal is not marginal growth, but to make them great. The time you put in should be worth the investment. I am not suggesting they should have a goal of $400,000 in the first year—but be aggressive!

Don't operate under the fear that they're going to get too good and move on. That's the wrong attitude. If they aren't good, why have them on your team at all? If they are good, they probably aren't going to be a junior broker forever, true. Help them in their career because it's the right thing to do, and you will get paid back for doing the right thing. That's not just my recommendation. That's based on conversations with very successful advisors who have cycled through several great junior brokers over many years.

Sales Managers

Whether you are managed by your broker-dealer or the bank, there is one person at the bank who is hopefully asking you, "What can I do to help?"

Do what the top people do, because another consistency I have seen from top-producing advisors is that they have great relationships with their sales managers. They consider the relationship an investment. You should, too. It's an investment in the firm you work for. It's an investment in the other advisors that make the bank's brand appealing. It's an investment in a favor when you need it.

Good sales managers do make note of what is working for other advisors and can often look objectively at your business and offer advice. When they ask what they can do to help, get the help! It may be something small like a budget for a client appreciation event—and a great relationship with them makes it a perfectly easy thing for them to approve. It may be something bigger, like giving you the better branches or paying for more sales assistants. Nurture that relationship just as you cultivate all your other relationships.

Wholesalers

If you want a steak dinner, take the steak dinner. But if you want to make more money and grow your business, go to your broker-dealer's national sales meeting and find the wholesaler who is attending sessions other than their own. Find the wholesaler who is taking notes during the technology session hosted by the broker-dealer. *That is the wholesaler who is interested in helping advisors grow their business.* They want to get in the weeds and help you mine your book for opportunities, and they are willing to learn. Today's wholesaler can be a valuable asset to your business.

Full disclosure: I have wholesaled for years. But having been an advisor and sales manager as well, I know the relationship from both sides of the desk. The bottom line I've observed is this: there is value in all relationships when you have the right attitude about them.

The wholesaling game has changed. Firms have gotten away from winning business purely through entertainment. Now, there's an expectation for wholesalers to become important members of your team by adding business-building value. Much like sales managers, there are varying levels of engagement, experience, and perspective.

The fact is that wholesalers have something you need, and that is product. You can do business with the company without ever meeting the wholesaler, but you will be missing out on the benefits of partnering with the wholesaler.

Create a calendar for when you will meet with wholesalers. Maybe you decide you will only have two meetings per week with wholesalers, and you only do it first thing in the morning. Just communicate that and avoid the cat-and-mouse sales process.

As we have discussed, share your business plan, incorporate the wholesalers into your client advocacy boards, your educational workshops, and perhaps into your referral training and staff appreciation events. Learn about product updates, get economic updates from them, and ask what competitors are giving them fits.

Ask directly what your wholesalers see other advisors do—advisors who produce more commissions or manage more assets than you. When you meet the right wholesalers (and they are out there), their partnership will weigh just as heavily in importance as the competitiveness of their products.

Explain your product shelf to the wholesaler and give them the opportunity to compete for your business. Be honest with them. Even if you know their product is better than what you are offering, but you don't want to switch just because you don't want to switch, just tell them that. Treat it as a business decision, and they will respect you for it.

Oh, and when they ask you to lunch, ask if you can bring a few good branch referrers. The wholesaler will be happy to help your business, and the staff appreciates the recognition and reward.

A Quick Personal Observation

I think there is something to be learned from this fact: during my time as a wholesaler, my best relationships have been with larger producers. It's not because I am only pursuing larger producers; wholesalers call on everyone. As a practical matter, this is how I got so many of them to share ideas for this book. But the larger producers respect my time, my budget, and my ideas, and they treat me like a partner—not a salesperson. I am guessing you see something similar in your relationships with your best clients. Draw whatever conclusion you want, but it is a trend.

Be Purposeful and Proactive

In the 10% of the time you spend planning your business, revisit your plans for utilizing your team. By this I mean clearly plan how you will gain time through the use of a team. Then plan how you will use that gained time. The gained time is how you grow your business.

Don't let the business happen *to* you. Make time for yourself to do the important business-building work. The structure you build and the hires you make, often in partnership with the bank, will play a huge role in your success and your job satisfaction. The best teams win.

CHAPTER 14

LICENSED BANKERS

Some banks have them and some don't, and by "them," I mean licensed bankers.

(If you don't have any licensed bankers in your organization, you can skip this chapter—or read on to determine whether it's something worth approaching the bank about.)

There are fewer licensed banker or LB programs now versus just a few years ago—simply because the regulatory environment has gotten stricter, especially when qualified assets are involved.

These LB programs can be a phenomenal asset to the advisor, but the key is understanding and leveraging the motivation of the program. Motivation is "why" the banks have LB programs. Some banks use them primarily as referral opportunities and prospectors for the advisors, and in that case, they are definitely a fantastic resource! Some use them as true agents to sell products, but from a limited basic list of products, and there, too, you have an opportunity. Some, although rare now, expect them to be nearly at a full advisor status—securities license and all.

The idea is that frontline staff, such as branch managers and new account representatives, are able to do very basic planning and cross-selling. If a client comes in to renew a CD, the new account rep they sit with will be licensed and able to make a sale without the need to refer the client over to a financial advisor. For the bank, there's no secret that it is about the bottom line: an LB program means more licenses, more touchpoints, more people with sales goals, and more clients of the bank purchasing products and creating revenue.

I have met many advisors who are certainly great at being advisors, but that doesn't always translate into their being good coaches for LBs. Similarly, I have met great sales managers or coaches of licensed bankers who would not be good advisors.

The fact is these are two different jobs that require different skill sets. You aren't trying to make the LBs good financial advisors. You are trying to grow them into good licensed bankers. To do so takes time, patience, and repetition. Remember that they probably did not come to the bank to be salespeople, and they probably didn't come to work at the bank to sell investments. But if you simplify the product list and the process, LBs can be very good.

In short, utilizing licensed bankers, although a time-intensive activity to incorporate into your business, can truly benefit you.

Full Disclosure

Some LB programs are competitive with what the advisor does, as you've already guessed. That is, assets do not go to your book of business, the advisor receives no compensation, etc. While that might seem like a deterrent to encourage and support the

LB program of your bank, there are still reasons you want to make it successful. Notably, when you properly position what you do, the bankers will learn when it's appropriate to refer to you versus when to write something themselves. I see this symbiosis regularly.

Alternatively, and to your advantage, there may be the opportunity to share commissions. You should do this when you have the opportunity (check with the bank's compliance department). The money the LBs stand to make for referring to you and sharing in your commissions is much better than the token referral fee they can make like anyone else in the bank. Consider that cost an investment in your business, and it will pay off.

If you have a program where LBs truly support the bank's financial advisors, then you should consider this one of your primary marketing strategies. It won't matter how few or how many LBs the bank certifies or employs—you can benefit. I would consider this among the most powerful and successful ways to leverage bank relationships and the bank environment.

As I said earlier, there are a number of potential moving parts because every bank runs the licensed banker program differently. Let me point out some of those moving parts here so that you consider all factors:

1. Compensation and Scorecards

It's important to understand the compensation plan because that provides some insight into both the bank's motivation in the program and the LBs' motivation. It comes down to this: how hard they might work for you depends on the compensation they get for doing so.

Always, always cut the LB in on commissions when you can. It makes great relationship- and referral-building sense: you will get a lot more referrals when the LBs share part of the commission! However, don't let them get paid if they truly haven't earned it. But when there's an opportunity, it helps engagement.

Another aspect of the LBs' life in the bank to consider, apart from but related to compensation, is the bank "scorecard." Banks usually have metrics in place for staff to do goal-setting and measure performance. This can be important since some LBs are simply going to be more motivated by their scorecard than they are by actual commissions. If they have their eye on that annual pay raise or a promotion, their scorecard numbers will be critical to them. Depending on the way the economic winds are blowing, the scorecard is also critical for job security.

2. Sales Versus Referral

Determine whether the LBs are actually making sales or if they are "referral only." And remember that they must be currently licensed so they can receive commissions based on the sale.

3. Licensing

What are the LBs licensed to do? Is it for securities and insurance, or for insurance only? In other words, what product menu are they licensed for? Where is there a referral opportunity?

4. Product Menu

The goal of the LBs' product menu should be simplicity, and, in fact, there is typically only a limited menu (compared to your own) for the LBs to work from. If it's insurance only, they usually have fixed annuities, with an occasional indexed annuity or a single premium wealth transfer life insurance product. If the LB holds a securities license, then it's usually a small stable of diversified retail mutual funds.

5. Management

Licensed Bankers will technically always report up through their bank branch manager. I have never seen advisors have true management responsibilities over any LB outside of coaching and training (and refer back to Chapter 3 on referral training for your role with the LB).

Many banks will have some version of sales manager responsible for LB sales. Although they are not the LBs' managers per se, there is a dotted line that gives them authority over the LBs. The sales manager will work with the branch manager in developing this facet of his responsibilities. Note: The number of LBs that this sales manager is responsible for can be a bellwether for how serious the bank is about the LBs actually making sales. I have seen anywhere from twenty LBs per manager to over a hundred.

If a sales manager has one hundred LBs, there is no real chance of the LB receiving individual developmental support. It's coaching with a broad brush, such as through conference calls only. That sales manager is instead usually busy maintaining licensing, getting new bankers licensed, making sure everyone is up-to-date on continuing education fulfillment, and similar tasks—not really doing individual sales training, product training, or any type of coaching. In this environment, it's much more common for the financial advisor to take over the bulk of the LB coaching, training, and motivating.

A sales manager with just twenty or thirty LBs will be doing much more one-on-one work, and there will be much larger expectations for consistent sales. This model is more typical if bankers are securities-licensed.

6. Coaching for Your Licensed Banker

I assume here that the bank is not going to be geared up for full-on LB continuous coaching and training. As a "hands-off"-coach or trainer, sometimes the best we can do is remove "road-blocks" that are either perceived or real for the LB. Here are some coaching, training, and support tactics to use with your LBs. Use one or more of them, but be careful not to overwhelm them.

Minimal initial product shelf. Give the LB an initial comfort level with only one or two products, then add a third one. Start with fixed annuities or a simple indexed annuity. An annuity is a natural product to transition to—safe, simple, and rate-driven. I call them the "safety scissors of the investment world." Keep reading to understand why three is the magic number.

Scripts and script practice. Create scripts for the LB for every phase of the meeting and sale. Simplify, simplify, simplify—make scripts using common language and a very repeatable process.

Transitioning during client meetings. One of the challenges I hear most frequently is that bankers are unsure how to *transition the conversation* from bank products to investment products. Here is the solution:

> Banker: "Have you thought about doing something better?"
>
> Client: "What would be better?" or "What does it pay?" (Usually some question suggested by your word "better.")
>
> Banker: "Well, let me ask you a few questions to see what would be better for you." (LB begins profiling questions.)

Profiling. You know this is the heart of your initial meetings with all prospects. Help the LB by giving him a basic profile format to use. I know you probably aren't accustomed to using a profiling form yourself, but it's not a bad idea for LBs. Again, it gives them the comfort of a structure and a script to go from. It ensures that the required information is collected in order to make an appropriate recommendation.

You would be surprised (as I still am) to know that an inexperienced banker—maybe like you, early in your career—can get all the way through a presentation on a five-year product and get to the point where the client is raising some objections … only to find out that the client plans to spend the money in three years! It's pretty tough to overcome objections when you haven't profiled thoroughly enough to match an investment with a need.

Objections. List the common ones and train the LB how to deal with them—before the client brings any of them up. You will know what they are, but the LB won't necessarily know until they have significant experience dealing with real clients.

Closing. Remember that LBs are not used to closing a sale. The very instruction "Close them!" might stir up fear. They have never closed on a CD or any other products. They will need some specific wording that they are comfortable with, so again, make sure they have scripts:

The most benign: "Does that sound good?" (If the customer says yes, then start the paperwork.)

A bit more directive: "Having worked in the bank for X years, I have worked with a lot of people in a similar situation, and I think you should do the annuity. Shall we do that?"

A financial planning process. When an LB gets into basic planning with a client (and they will), train them to simplify in their presentation to clients . . . just as you do. Have them use something as simple as a three-bucket approach with memorable labels:

- *"Daily Dollars"* bucket (three to six months' worth of living expenses): "This is the money you use at the grocery store—leave this in your checking account."

- *"Emergency Money"* bucket (six to twelve months' worth of living expenses): "This is in case your car breaks down or you need a new air conditioning system—leave this in a money market or CD."

- *"Rainy Day Money"* bucket (the rest): "This is all your other money, and you don't know when you will need it. Maybe you'll never need it. I can help you do *better* with this money."

This gives the LB a basic structure or process for how money fits into someone's life—for how to discuss financial preparedness with clients. It provides scripted scenarios for the LB to refer to with the client and better prepares the LB for the presentation and objections.

For instance, the LB can now state in memorable, everyday language that both he and the client can follow, "If we identify this money is Rainy Day Money, then we shouldn't worry about liquidity. That's why we have the other buckets. With this Rainy Day bucket, we should try to get a better rate—and a CD isn't good enough for that." The client will go home and mimic your words to his spouse: "Honey, we need to decide how to do better with our Rainy Day Money!"

Options versus recommendations. From my experience, many LBs are more comfortable giving a few *options*, since they don't typically have the confidence to make a definitive *recommendation*. And that's totally okay! Make sure the LB stays with at most three options. As I've stated elsewhere, giving too much product information to the client in one meeting is like sniffing too many perfume samples at the department store—you start to swoon, and you don't remember what any particular scent smelled like.

A Final Training Tip

Have your licensed banker walk through three options with *as many* clients as he possibly can, whatever the initial purpose of the meeting with the client. It's practice! Step #1 to train the LB on a small/medium/large approach. It could be a CD/Fixed Annuity/Indexed Annuity trio. It could be the CD/Annuity/Wealth Transfer trio. The key is that there are just three options. Step #2 is real-time practice with real clients. The LB can preface it with a statement like, "I know you came in for a CD, but let me just show you the other things that many of my clients are doing when they want to keep their money very safe," or, "We have a financial advisor here that can help you, but before you meet with them, let me show you the top three things that I help my clients with." The client doesn't feel pressured or should not—only educated! And the LB is, in effect learning by putting on a teacher hat— they gain confidence on presenting and eliminating objections to three products, through repetition that educates the client.

Although they actually have more than three sizes, Starbucks consistently advertises its core three sizes of beverage. Whether it is a cold drink, a specialty drink, or their plain ol' coffee-of-the-day, they ask, "Will that be a tall, grande, venti for you?" Just those three options. There is a psychology of sales and buying, which tells Starbucks that the consumer will lean toward the middle or "grande" option. If there are two sizes larger than a small, then the small must be too small, but the large must be for heathens!

More encouragement for the LBs:

Let the LBs Set Goals

Starting out, let LBs set their production and referral goal while you agree to hold them accountable for achievement. Give them tips along the way. This will help them buy into the goal. Alternatively, when goals are set for the LB by the bank, your role to the LB is still to help them reach that goal.

When you have an LB who is really struggling or new to the business, set goals for the number of sales or applications signed. This will take the focus off the premium or gross commissions and put the focus on the *process* of making sales. They may feel more comfortable with small trades. You would rather, in fact, that they get their feet wet by practicing on small opportunities and encourage them to refer large opportunities to you if they feel insecure.

The key to any goal setting is the follow-up—*your* follow-up. The "inspect what you expect" rule applies. You can make it a formal review, but frame it as help to them, like this:

> "Let's plan on connecting on the phone every Tuesday morning, just to see how it's going for you. We can talk over any objections you are having a hard time with, or product details that might help you."

Joint Appointments and Modeling

Joint appointments and modeling can be great for encouraging referrals and helping the LB understand the full scope of what you do. Model or demonstrate to the LB your holistic planning, low-pressure sales process and scripting, relationship-building tactics, etc.

You have to be careful not to scare them into the "I will never be able to do that" mentality. Be their teacher and trainer. Break it into bite-sized chunks for them, and present one chunk per appointment with them. Take a few opportunities to model for them the sales process they are being trained on. When they see it done correctly, then they'll be able to do it themselves with confidence.

CHAPTER 15

CLIENT APPRECIATION EVENTS

It is often talked about and even planned for, but rarely executed: the client appreciation event.

I can feel some of you cringing. Some of you are paging through to the next chapter.

But stop! This client appreciation event tactic to build business probably isn't what you think it is.

As far as more marketing activity options go, I know advisors in your position that have absolutely built their business through client appreciation events. Done correctly, the events:

- garner referrals.

- build relationships of trust.

- get you more assets.

Clients get excited by the next scheduled event, and they even become a sought-after social event for people who may not have busy schedules. It really is a great way for bank clients to meet others from their community with mutual interests!

If you are worried that no one will show up for your party, I get it—but take a leap of faith. Do one event (however small), and the second will be easier (and larger) than the first. The third will be easier (with more attendees) than the second. And then you'll be off, running fun, productive events!

Often thought of for fee-only advisors and book brokers only, they can be used by anyone. Even if it's your first year in the bank (when you most desperately need to market yourself), *these events work*.

For fee-based advisors and book brokers (advisors who just work their book of business and don't actually cover branches), these events are critical. If you were an advisor in 2008, you already understand that. Advisors lost clients when they didn't have deep *relationships* that were based on more than just rates of return.

But since then, too, with the rise of discount brokerages (which are really a front for gathering managed money) and robo-advisors, there are a hundred places your clients could do it for cheaper. When the market is going up, it's easy to justify fees. But when the market is going down (it will again, eventually), and you are *the* person to help them preserve their accumulated wealth, you need to have a compelling reason to make them stay with you or seek you out. A *relationship* of trust and expertise may be the only way to achieve that. Your chances of a good relationship rise exponentially if you have hosted the client at a client appreciation event.

What to Do and How to Do It

Like "old-school seminars," I am not a fan of steak dinner events. Loud, obnoxious, and impersonal, they will not get you any kind of bang for your buck.

But restaurant locales for your event do work when your choice of restaurant is judicious. Make it a hometown favorite— somewhere that has a great reputation in the community or is known for a particular atmosphere. To generalize, our client base is middle America. Let's face it: most of us are more comfortable with everyday familiar surroundings than a stuffy, high-end restaurant we would only go to once every five years for an anniversary dinner with our spouse. At a well-chosen venue, you can arrange for the chef or owner to come out and talk about how they make their award-winning macaroni and cheese or have one of the venue's signature cocktails made and the recipe explained to your guests by their bartender. That makes it more of an "event" than just a typical dinner.

Who to Invite

Of course, you invite clients. This is a client appreciation event. Your A-list clients are at the top of the guest list. If you aren't already segmenting your book, it's time to start. These guests are your A-listers and are the clients that you either already have, or individuals or couples you plan to turn into full-fledged financial planning clients.

Other guests might include:

- Key management from the bank, even if it's just one individual. In the clients' eyes, this ties you to the bank and its brand.

- Your team members: sales assistant(s), junior brokers, key licensed bankers. Invite them in a rotation if you have a big team. You don't want more staff than clients at the event!

- Your spouse and children, if age-appropriate. I am even a fan of inviting your parents if possible. It makes you seem like just "a family from our town."

- Timely prospects. Got prospects with big money who are still kicking the tires? Send all of them an invitation to be your personal guest. They get exposure to you and other bankers (and with other clients of yours), no strings attached. This can help them develop the comfort they need to realize that they *do* trust you enough to talk money!

Do Some Talking

If you don't address the group, you are missing a key opportunity. Be so well-prepared that you don't need notes (or don't need to refer to them too much). Introduce your spouse, your team, and any bank employees.

Thank clients for their business. Stress that it is important to you and that you understand the importance of the trust they are placing in you and that you don't take it lightly.

Thank all those present for the referrals they have provided to you—do this *even* if no one has—and that you are happily working with those referred clients now.

Consider giving a brief economic update, presented either by you or by a wholesaler. This gives the wholesaler a great reason to be there, which they may be required to do if they are paying for it. Keep any single talk to no more than five minutes because this is a fun event, not a business meeting.

Close the event by reminding the attendees what you do and your differentiators (review Chapter 6 on branding), which by now you have nicely packaged.

Funding the Event

Never let money be a reason not to hold this event. While it's not all about keeping it inexpensive, it doesn't have to be overly expensive. There are plenty of reasonably priced options out there.

The bank may have a marketing budget you can use. Your broker-dealer might contribute. If you have wholesalers you are loyal to, they might contribute. In the worst-case scenario, you might come out of pocket for it, but it's a great investment in your business.

Design the Event Creatively

Think of something you know your clients would enjoy or something you enjoy that you would like to introduce them to. Possibilities are endless. Food and beverage, and by extension, restaurants, are always a good bet to please a crowd in our culture. But there are other unique options that will be more memorable:

- A cooking class taught by a chef

- A wine, beer, or bourbon tasting, which is especially nice if you live in or near a growing or producing region (check with your bank and broker-dealer for compliance guidelines with alcohol)

- A tour of a museum, stadium, etc.

- A hobby-related lesson (fly-tying, horseback riding, quilting, jewelry-making, etc.)

- Renting a movie theater for a private showing

- Renting a whole bowling alley for a few hours

- Inexpensive sporting events

- A play at a theater

Consider Bringing In an Expert

You can hold some of your client appreciation events in your work environment, too. Don't exclude this option. Somewhere in the bank, there will be a conference room or training room you can use to host up to fifteen or twenty people.

For instance: pay a local golf pro to come in for an hour. He'll tell the story of the year they were on the tour, followed by presenting a short game clinic for attendees. Even a non-golfing client might get excited to bring a few of their golfing friends. If you are in a music-oriented town, a version of this could be a local musician who tells a story about a concert, then gives a "music appreciation clinic" for ten minutes or so. Or is your town big into high school football or basketball? Be in tune with your community, get inspired by its local passions, then use one of those as an event theme.

You provide snacks, coffee, and water. Perhaps invite ten or twenty clients and tell them each to bring a friend or two who they regularly enjoy leisure activities with. Raffle something off—a sand wedge for golf, etc. Hit up wholesalers for related swag bags, so that everyone goes home with something. Even people not really devoted to the topic of the meeting can get inspired and excited—and feel your gratitude!

What's in It for Your Business?

You spend an afternoon or evening with "A" clients, maybe meet another ten or twenty people—your clients' own guests—who are probably a lot like your clients. You have minimal expenses. You walk away with no one knowing that you're terrible at golf (or whatever the theme happened to be that time), all the while deepening or initiating relationships of trust.

Try it once, and you will see why the big producers do these events. They aren't as daunting as they sound. In fact, even if you do despise golfing or theater, you will also have fun.

CHAPTER 16

COVERING MULTIPLE BRANCHES

As financial advisors hired by banks with many branch offices per region, we are often assigned the responsibility of covering or servicing a number of branches. It could be anywhere from a couple to far too many branches. Being handed such an opportunity to do more business is both a blessing and a curse.

Why More Is Not More

We have a responsibility to be present in each of the branches we are assigned to, and when there are far too many, we are cursed with time and people-management challenges. The blessing? We have a business need—to develop our clientele—and covering more than one branch opens us to a larger pool of clients.

Ultimately, though, as you build a strong business, you will cut back. You do so as more advisors are added by the bank (because of your success? I hope so!) or when you decide that you want to cover fewer branches. But when and if you cut back is very dependent on the market, your personal and the bank management's revenue expectations, etc.

I have seen advisors assigned to a single branch. But I've also seen advisors assigned to as many as twenty. Sometimes the banks are very close in proximity, so you can understand their rationale for the clustering. But sometimes, the branches are spread across a large area or even multiple states, and that is not as easy to execute on or rationalize. Often, it's just making the best of the geography according to the sales manager's best efforts. Unless you are a genius at time and team management, having many branches spread across a territory, requiring you to be in a car or even on a plane often, will not really be a lucrative practice. Not for you. Not for the bank. But, again, banks do it, and we adapt as best we can. This is the curse.

When Less Is More

This maxim is as uncomfortable as it is true in our business: "When you are someone to everyone, then you are someone to no one."

You can actually get more out of five branches than ten branches. Why? Because you are someone to five branches. You are no one when you have ten of them.

Relying on low-hanging fruit from more branches is a sucker's bet. The quality of leads will not be as good. I guarantee it!

You have to build a strategy allowing you to cover all your assigned branches. You need a strategy both to maximize time, teammates, opportunity—and to fulfill your formal goals. Some advisors, however, do not do this purposefully, and it ends up running and ruining their business. I send you back to Chapter 12 on writing up a business plan.

This said, there is no secret to those who've tried servicing twenty branches: you can really only effectively cover four to six branches, tops. By "effectively cover," I mean to be fully engaged and involved *while developing serious long-term business.* Knowing everyone, attending meetings without fail, effectively training to build referrals, and building meaningful relationships are all vital activities since (must I remind you?) we are in a people business.

Don't be fooled by your or your bank management's possible "more is better" mentality. At the core of that thinking is a scarcity mindset. Banks think that there are few "real clients" for you in any individual branch—and so they assign more branches to you, thinking they are doing you a favor. They also think that if they only have one (or few) financial advisors roaming the branches, it costs them less.

Let that go. Take on fewer branches when given the choice. There is plenty of money out there in the "less is more" scenario!

This said, for those of you assigned many branches, I can share some tactics that will help you 1) develop long-term business relationships with bank employees and clients in all the branches, and 2) prevent you from having a nervous breakdown while doing it.

Your Key Metrics to Design Strategy

When you cover many branches, you don't want to have to guess which clients at each branch represent the best prospects for your business. To decide who is and who is not a valuable investment of your time, you need data.

The bank possesses that data. You just need to get it. Your rationale to management when requesting data is that it will help you craft "a more revenue-productive approach."

The key information you need that's vital for planning your territory—and get it for each branch—is the *branch deposits*. Next, gather information about account types and deposit amounts. Find out how much is in IRAs, CDs, money markets, savings accounts, personal checking and business accounts. Some of these data points don't provide as much opportunity as others, and I have listed them in descending order for what I would consider offering the most potential.

Why getting data is key is further illustrated specifically by the branches' *business* accounts. If it's a $50,000 operating account, it's probably not a good lead for that money, although it could still be a good lead to the business owner. A business account with $3,000,000 may be a great lead, as the business owner may have just been stacking up excess cash because they're not sure what else to do with it. That could be a very good lead for that money.

The goal is to use the data you end up with to drive your activity, your relationship-building, and your time allotments. By convincing bank management that possessing this data will help you drive more revenue to the bank, a smart manager will give you the access you need.

Other Branch Metrics

Another way this data is critical is that deposits drive the number of employees, the size of a physical branch, the foot traffic, other departments' presence, and a plethora of in-house goals, etc.

An average deposit base per advisor varies from one bank to the next, but on average in banks, it is $100M–$300M. In credit unions, it's usually $250M–$500M. The disparity exists because of the less-developed sales culture in credit unions.

When More Is Better

There are a number of variables in play, but as a rule, I wouldn't spend too much time at branches under $50M, but spend significant time at branches over $100M. If you have a branch with over $250M in deposits, I would make a case for never leaving the branch, although those branches usually exist only in the really large banks. Thus, the more in deposits a branch has, the more interest it holds for you as a pool of clients.

As a rule of thumb, for every $1 deposited, each client has $3–$4 dollars somewhere else. Thus, if you have a $100 million branch, that bank's clients collectively own $400–$500 million in assets . . . somewhere. If your branches total $250 million, you are potentially fishing from a pool of a billion dollars. And that's a lot of money!

Just a quick reminder: if you can add $10–$20 million a year to your book of business, you will be wildly successful.

To give you some additional perspective, many investment programs' deposit penetration is 1%–2% annually (that is, the number of deposits that will be converted into new investment products every year). Three percent of deposit penetration is considered very *effective*, while *the most effective* investment programs and advisors in the country are in the 5%–6% range.

A Hub-and-Spoke Strategy

If you have more than six branches assigned to you, you need to create a hub-and-spoke model. The hub is:

- your central base of operations

- where you will spend significant time (but perhaps not most of your time, and certainly not all of it)
- geographically convenient to most or all the other "spoke" branches

Ideally, your "hub" should be the largest deposit branch of those assigned to you. However, let geography be an important criterion before you select your hub. If there is a smaller branch that is very convenient to several or all others, you may make the smaller one your hub for travel-time savings. You may have one or more hubs depending on how many branches you cover and the geography.

All other branches are the "spokes" of that wheel. You should always plan to visit spoke branches on a scheduled rotation for training and large or important meetings, but it may not be a branch that you will commit purposeful time or effort in developing after looking at the data points we've just discussed. That is, focus on building relationships in the hub branch, as that effort creates more opportunity than smaller branches because of these metrics.

Rule #1 for Your Spoke Branches

Don't ignore them!

If any branch manager feels you are ignoring his location, you will get nothing from their staff: no referrals, no recognition, no kind of support. Set a realistic expectation of visits-on-rotation and stick to it. Communicate clearly to the manager about when to expect you. Refer back to building your business plan and reviewing it with key people if this isn't making sense *right now*.

To reduce your driving time, consider virtual meetings. Video conferences still allow people to see your face or hear your voice; you can nurture relationships through video. Holding such conferences shows staff you are committed despite the difficulties of needing to serve many branches. When they see that you know how to hustle and are doing your best for their clientele, support will increase.

Getting Started

For the first year or two, you will have to drive. You simply have to be where the money is at all times and show that you are putting in the effort to service the branch's clients, to build your book, and to make a living. That is the bottom line.

Staying Consistent—Have a Clear Written Strategy

Clearly, at some point, you have to control and run your business with a predetermined strategy. Otherwise, your business will run and ruin you. Letting yourself be pulled all over your branch assignment area haphazardly without a strategy will not work long-term. Thoughtfully make the transition into a documented plan for serving all your hub-and-spoke locations.

Here are some ideas to run your multi-branch business much more smoothly:

- Communicate your plan vertically in the bank. (Refer back to Chapter 12.)

- Share your calendar with everyone you can, but especially with each branch manager. Be transparent to them about where you will be working on any given day; a manager should know when to expect you at their location.

- Remember that most bankers are tied to their desks for eight hours a day, so when you leave the branch at 2 p.m. to go to another, others will just assume you are going home for the day. Frankly, that might not make you so likable; be loud and clear about what you are doing, where you'll be doing it, and how long you'll "be over at branch X" today. Again, having it appear in your shared calendar explains your movements. It is also supported by your documented strategic plan.

- Do some high-level profiling over the phone to rule out poor leads. (But don't start selling!)

- Do more group referral training rather than individual coaching, whether in person or virtually and institute a Branch Referral Advocacy program. (Refer back to Chapter 3.)

- Hire junior advisors to chase smaller accounts and do service appointments and reviews. Book time for training and support. (See Chapter 13.)

- Leverage licensed bankers for prospecting and gathering initial information. (See Chapter 14.)

At some point, you'll realize that your time in your office is more valuable than any time in the car. This is quite hard for new or smaller producers to imagine, because if there is a chance to get in front of any money, they will do it! But a drive between branches may mean not making the phone calls to the kinds of clients and prospects you need to hit higher production levels.

Covering Your Branches

Proper coverage of your branches is of paramount importance. *Do it right!*

Covering assigned branches the right way—i.e., with a written strategic plan that you consistently implement, and a calendar shared with branch managers—will not necessarily make you, but doing it wrong will break you. Trying to cover too many branches in a helter-skelter manner is a leading indicator of future failure. Too many times I've seen this happen.

Get the data on your assigned branches. Divide into a hub-and-spoke formation and conquer. Use your remote conferencing tools. Develop, train, and use a team. Let success happen, just like you let sales happen: by implementing a well-designed, data-supported methodical strategy. Hopefully, you're seeing the pieces of the puzzle fit together!

CHAPTER 17

YOUR OFFICE

This is a rather mundane topic, you say? It's nonetheless well worth discussing. Why? I have been in hundreds and hundreds of advisors' offices, and I can say that many could be doing it better!

While we are ideally in the main branch (our hub) with dedicated office space, this is not always the case. When you go to your spoke branches, you likewise may have no assigned office—or even the same desk for every visit.

Meetings at a spoke branch that you cover may find you sitting at another banker's desk or office. If you can only use a desk and not an enclosed office, it is what it is. Accept with grace that the bank is not going to block expensive space for *you*, someone who's only in the branch one day every two weeks. It just won't make economic sense to them. Be grateful you have at least the desk space! *

The bank may have an available enclosed space for you: a conference room, training room, board room, or break room. Don't complain about where they put you, or you won't be welcomed back. Your space may be not ideal, but you'll have to make do.

If you are kicking someone out of their office every time you come to have a meeting, be very gracious about it. Be so nice about it that they look forward to it. Find out what their favorite candy or coffee is and bring them a treat. If that manager or employee is upset that every time their branch gives you a referral, they have to go sit in the chilly break room while you use their office or desk, then you won't get many referrals. Make it as comfortable for them as you can.

If it's a really big appointment, it might be worth inviting the individual to your home branch if it's not too far out of the way. That gives you an edge since you can properly set the stage. It's still their bank—the brand they know and trust—and it's where they are comfortable and familiar. But if they decline and prefer their local branch, again, be gracious about it and accept. You do want to focus on coming to the client at his local branch as often as you need. As your success grows and you become busier, you will cut back on this. Also, as you become better known to some of your longer-term clients, they might agree to come to your hub office for future meetings with you.

Understand the Power of Perception

As you know, where you hold meetings is not always in your control. Nor are the prospect or client's perceptions of your surroundings. Perceptions have huge subconscious power and can make or break the meeting. I mean that if you have carefully choreographed your "space," you can comfort the client, and his perceptions will be on the positive side. If you act uncomfortable about the space or speak disparagingly about it, the clients will feel uncomfortable as well, and they will have a negative perception ... of *you*.

Put yourself in their shoes: if your surroundings seem temporary (or you act like they are), then you, too, seem temporary. If you seem uncomfortable, they will be, too. Discomfort doesn't breed trust; it damages your trust and credibility.

Manage their perceptions about your temporary space and their fear that you are just a guy passing through with no stake in outcomes. Your temporary meeting space creates the opportunity for you to explain—*and this is important*—that this is not your home branch or your home base, *but you want to make it easier for clients in this neighborhood to come in and visit with you.*

You will say something like, "I spend most of my day at X branch (downtown, in X city) because they frankly have more office space. They are also centrally located, so I can easily make it to your branch to be convenient for you."

This type of matter-of-fact statement will also set the stage for the hub-and-spoke model we discussed earlier. It will help you set expectations on your availability and location. They'll see that you have made the drive to them, and they'll appreciate the effort. Also, when they see enough value in what you provide, they will gladly drive to you for a future appointment you set together. They will think no more about the drive to you than their drive three towns over to see a specific doctor.

No matter where you meet with your client, make it as professional as possible. Manage perception by sitting in the client's chair and really, really look around the space. What needs to be picked up, put away, dusted off, organized in a neat pile, turned off, or hidden? Do it. If you have a TV in the space, turn it off.

More Perceptions: Your Home Base Office

I have walked into advisors' offices and thought that it was just a temporary space, only to find out it was their permanent office. So, next, pay good attention to perceptions in your formally assigned space in your hub branch. Assuming you have a place to call your own, show your degrees and certifications on the wall. (Unless, perhaps, you are baby-faced and just graduated college. Do not confirm their suspicion that you graduated college last month.) But those certificates on the wall are a great way to give the client the message that you were serious enough about your career to get the education for it. Look around the doctor's office next time; they do it, too.

Most importantly, make it looked lived in. Bring in some pictures of the kids or the dogs or your spouse. This said, go easy on your office display of awards from your broker-dealer and product vendors (aka Industry Glass). They smell of "salesman" or "saleswoman." You don't want them to feel they are about to be "sold" something. Or worse: you present a product from a company for which they see eight awards on the credenza! Then they might feel like you aren't personalizing their plan but instead giving everyone the same product, no matter what.

Display anything that will tie you to your client or make you seem familiar. For instance, if you are in a town where there is a John Deere factory, then have a small toy John Deere tractor on your desk or a John Deere ballcap on the back counter. If it comes up in conversation, then you can explain how your sister (dad, aunt, grandfather) worked there, or how so many of your clients have worked there. This gives you credibility and connects you to the community.

Can they see your computer screen? Well, they should! Why? It serves to demystify the process. As an aside, don't let the computer screen be a distraction during your conversations. If you are filling out paperwork or opening an account online with them, then it can be useful.

Be cognizant of books, magazines, and literature in your office, and think about the perception they create. Don't have anything sales-related laying around. "He's selling me!" is a big client fear! Financial planning or finance titles are fine for books on a library-type shelf, but *no* finance industry magazines.

Think about it: professional golfers don't look for tips in golf magazines. Likewise, you should not be giving the impression that you are looking for wealth-management tips in *Money* magazine.

If you have a lobby or waiting area, focus on lifestyle magazines (home and garden, sports, or travel topics are fine). This should inspire them to think about life while you take care of their money.

Confidentiality and Other Rookie Mistakes

Confidentiality is about "secrecy." You don't reveal information; you keep it secret and protected. Here is what to beware of:

- Don't leave client files or any notes from previous meetings out where others can see them.

- Don't have one of those traditional "phone message" slips of paper on top of the desk with a client name on it.

- Don't have a phone conversation during your meeting with Harold Smith and address Jean White on the phone by name. *Oh, he advises her?* Smith might think. *I* know *her!* Or worse, he'll think you reveal who your clients are so easily and will be less likely to want to work with you.

This all seems like common sense, but I see it all the time—people are private about money. Very, very private. Even their name being known is a breach of privacy.

Manage perceptions. Keep all client information 100% secure and confidential. It's about the space, but more about your behavior.

CHAPTER 18

CREDIT UNION ADVISORS

I know I have been using the term "bank" as all-encompassing to bank and credit union advisors in these pages. I ask again that you please excuse the brevity. I absolutely do recognize the critical differences, as I have worked exclusively with credit union advisors at times in my career. I know the division and the differences in culture, both real and perceived.

All of the topics, challenges, and tips given in these pages to "bank" advisors apply to credit union advisors, too, rest assured. But there are some extra things to know about working in credit unions that I'll address here.

Get the Language Right

The first and most obvious is the vernacular:

- The people you advise are "members," not clients or customers. Always members. If you have been in a credit union for more than five minutes, you already know that. This is a credit union's distinctive approach.

- Select employee groups are called SEG or "seg groups." The original group of people that the credit union was founded on is that "seg group," and it might be teachers, firefighters, military, phone company employees, or another clearly unique group. The credit union also may have added several more seg groups over time. Many CUs are now community-based with much more relaxed membership requirements in order to obtain more members and stay competitive with banks. Some are not and still require affiliation with particular professional groups. Either way, you may still see trends toward the original group of members.

- Share accounts. Every CU has different verbiage on what they call "accounts," but "share accounts" is a standard in the credit union market. They were originally called share accounts to represent "a financial share in the credit union," as they are owned by their members.

Get Your Approach Aligned

Here are a few things I know about credit union members that advisors would be wise to take into account:

- They may be slightly more conservative than the mainstream bank customer.

- They are slightly more fee- and risk-averse. That's likely how they became credit union members. They were looking for a free checking account or a lower loan rate.

- They are sometimes (but do not assume this without probing) less investment-savvy. This is not derogatory to them! It's not that they aren't smart—in fact, they are excellent teachers, police force employees, and members of our armed forces. But as a generalization, it is a matter of having obtained less financial and investment knowledge and experience.

I mention these slight differences as *they make for excellent opportunities for an advisor.*

Next, there are a few key tactics to leverage to be of service to this clientele:

Leverage Through a Service Approach

Low-pressure sales is important in the Credit Union philosophy. A service approach equals a low- to no-pressure sales strategy. They don't want to think that their Credit Union is selling them things and trying to make money off of them. Rather, these are additional services and products being *provided* to the Credit Union members.

Always thank them at each encounter (meeting, appointment, attendance at one of your events) for their membership. Include in your front talk that investment services are a *service* offered by the Credit Union to members. Say things like, "Our member's financial life is important to the Credit Union."

This service approach heightens your responsibility as a partner of the Credit Union in that you are expected to provide good service. It's critical in your relationship with the Credit Union that you follow through on it.

The service mentality is especially useful in referral training you will be conducting with Credit Union frontline bankers. You can beneficially emphasize the service mentality and not the sales mentality, saying to CU staff that "I can't *help* our members if I can't get in front of them."

Hold Educational Workshops

Taking an educational approach at most of your client events is really another service (and be sure to review Chapter 2 on this tactic). In appointments, a few extra minutes on educating people on relevant topics, and using the risk continuum (review that process in Chapter 9), goes a long way in materializing your low-pressure sales strategy, strengthening the relationship with the member, and helping them buy the way they want to buy.

Often the Credit Union has educational sessions for members on other business lines, such as debt counseling or buying a first home. Sometimes it is easy to advertise your workshops alongside other CU workshops, and you can leverage the success they have had in those workshops even if those business lines are unrelated to yours. Be sure to include statements like, "This is why I enjoy working in XYZ Credit Union. We take great pride in educating our members and it's not about trying to sell you something." This is assuming you are taking my advice on doing non-product-related workshops!

Borrow Trust

People trust their Credit Unions. Polls have shown they are consistently among the most trusted of all financial institutions. You can borrow that trust to build great relationships very quickly. Be sure at every possible opportunity that you are incorporating the Credit Union philosophy and its brand into your conversations.

Do Investment Program Co-Branding

Many Credit Unions have already done program co-branding, but in case yours hasn't, you should suggest that they do so. For example, if you work at XYZ Federal Credit Union, they can brand you as their *Investment Services Division*—even if you are a one-man shop. They will give it a name like XYZ Investment Services or XYZ Financial Services. You will need some help with this from the Credit Union, your broker-dealer and the marketing department. Be sure to check with the compliance and legal departments as well.

Communicate Your Personal Brand

As I discussed in the chapter about your personal brand as an advisor (you can refer back to Chapter 6), it's powerful to include something about the credit union in your personal brand. Still, you need to be able to communicate it in brief, well-articulated sentences that answer why you like that particular credit union, why you like the credit union movement, or why you are a good fit for working with whatever seg groups dominate the membership base.

Being important to the credit union is sometimes a challenge. It may be difficult to get support, resources, and attention. Lots of CU advisors have told me, "The credit union doesn't care about me. They don't do anything to support my business." In most cases, what that tells me is that the advisor is *not making them any money*—or not enough money to be on the CU's radar scope. While the CU is a not-for-profit entity, they are nonetheless a business. Thus, if you make them enough money to get noticed, then you will get more support and more attention. You will become a more primary business line.

The CU environment makes the other steps outlined in this book even more important (such as the business planning) since you will need to show them what you can do with just a few resources. As you prepare your plan and approach management for more resources, consider if it's administrative help, website space, seminar marketing, or a list to call from that you need.

You might experience some of the proverbial chicken-or-the-egg scenario at first. But keep at it! You may not make enough money to get more resources or support, but you can't make more money until you get those resources. Work with your sales manager or broker-dealer to sell this to credit union management. They have a vested interest in member service, and it's even more powerful if you control the narrative. Sell both the economic impact potential you have to the credit union (the fact that investment services are one of the stickiest account types), but also the importance of the service to members. If nothing else, if management has come to understand the poor financial planning decisions that some members make, it can win you their support.

Your brand, your professionalism, and your relationship with the credit union are imperative. Make it abundantly clear that you want to be part of their team, you want to contribute to the credit union, you want to help more members, and you want to help them buy more ATM machines and build more branches to better serve members.

Help management understand in net revenue terms what you will contribute, and that the stated revenue is a measure of *how many members* you have served.

Even very successful programs get member penetration in the low single digits as a percentage of total members. Use that! I have said to credit union CEOs, "Things are going well, but we are *only* serving 2% of your membership base." That should get their attention. Your broker-dealer should be able to help you determine your number of clients if you don't already know it.

The number of members that your credit union has is available on the NCUA website.

It will take time. Gains may feel marginal at first. Go for the cumulative outcomes: small gains add up. It will happen if you are consistent in this approach of constantly selling the importance of the program to your credit union (or to your bank, for that matter). Eventually you will have everything you need. And then ... it's on you!

In short, the credit union environment is a great place for building a financial planning practice. Many of the most successful advisors I have met are in credit unions, and they have tremendous job satisfaction. They say it is because they get members coming back to them relating how much they benefited from the services and education they provided!

The strategy is always the same, whether in traditional banking or the credit union environment: provide great service and education, develop meaningful relationships that last, build trust, and set high goals for yourself.

CONCLUSION

That's the recipe. Just as the tastiest dishes don't necessarily require heaps of hard-to-find ingredients, the best-run businesses succeed and thrive from taking a small number of actions—important actions—and doing them well:

- Prospecting and getting more appointments

- Selling in the way that the prospect or client wants to buy

- Running an efficient business so it scales activity and results.

Can't? Or won't? The most successful people, the ones who earn the most money, do something that others either *can't* do or *won't* do. I'm guessing that if you're reading this, then you're no Tom Brady or Venus Williams. You can't do what they do. That leaves you with doing what others *will not*. And success comes not from one-time actions but from consistency and purpose.

As I said from the start, there's no need to employ *all* of the tactics I present in this book. I would like you to realize, though, that the advisors who have gotten to the results you would also like to achieve—the advisors who have become top producers in our industry—have chosen one, two, or three business-building tactics from among the ones I present. *They mastered them.* They treat them as critical activities they must perform to achieve their stellar results.

Here's a secret. Something no one says about this business is that it's just another version of a blue-collar job.

How so? Well, imagine working at a factory to make widgets, over and over and over. You'd have to fine-tune your proprietary widget-making process:

- You'd find the production process that works best for you. (Your Business Plan)

- You'd get just the right number of people on the line. (Your Team)

- You'd give people the right on-the-job training. (Referral and Other Training)

- You'd test and select final tools from all the best machine tools available on the market. (Your Prospecting Tactics and Events)

- Every day, you'd repeat that process—and you'd get good at it, over and over, day after day. (Making a sale daily. Consistency. A solid forty-hour week!)

As a financial advisor, your "factory" is a bank or a credit union. The whole process is perfectly planned: excellently staffed, well-oiled, smooth, repeatable, and simplified. Effective.

It's a simple business, but not an easy business. It is the need to consistently perform according to your business plan that makes this profession the wrong fit for some people.

The quality of financial advice varies from one top producer to the next. Let me say this another way: the *quality* of advice is not the primary driver to an advisor's success at growing the business. That's hard for some people to understand. It's important, but not the primary driver.

That's a bitter reality for many of you who really enjoy the analytics involved in financial planning with clients. Yes, you should take great pride and care in giving your clients the best advice you are capable of giving. Yes, you must treat their money like you would your own family's money. But recognize that the most successful advisors are the ones who are the best at attracting a regular flow of new clients, retaining the clients they've gained, and gathering more assets over time from those clients.

A Few More Personal Words of Advice

Treat this as a business rather than a 9–5 job. Call it a business. Run it like a business. *The fact is that no one is going to take more interest in your business than you.*

Great results are not going to get handed to you. Reaching your goals won't happen overnight, but you will be surprised by how quickly it can be done. Be aggressive but realistic about the time it will take you. If you grossed $250,000 last year, then shoot for $500,000 next year. Go ahead and double it. If you did $500,000 last year, then aim for $750,000 next year. Bump it up 50%. Either goal is feasible by leaning on and using your selection of new business-building, sales-making tactics.

Don't set piker goals. I have had a lot of advisors who have just come off a $250,000 gross revenue year tell me their new goal for the coming year is … $275,000. *What?! That's for pikers!* That is decidedly *not* what I meant when I said to be realistic!

First, we both know that the growth in your managed-money book or trailed business can account for a significant portion of that revenue growth. Secondly, we both know that's one good trade. Don't set your goal for an entire year to be a measly one trade better than the prior year.

Get over the obstacles you have created in your mind and set a real goal. I have yet to see an advisor setting a "goal" for $275,000 who has ended the year at $500,000. You know why, don't you? We slam on the breaks. It's a self-fulfilling prophecy. Or even worse, we don't want to grow too fast, because then, we say our sales manager will *expect* that continued growth.

Pikers!

Also, decide what money means to you. By this, I mean to ask yourself what your own money means to you. Very few people can do this work just for the great paycheck. What does that earned money mean to you? Focus on that. It may be paying for your kids' tuition for a private school or funding their college later. It might allow you and the family to take extended exotic vacations every year. It could be donating to a beloved charity. It could be setting you up for your desired early retirement.

What do you really, really value that money can bring you, or at least help materialize? Helping others achieve financial success is great, but for most advisors, it doesn't pack enough caffeine to get you out of bed at 5 a.m. It's okay to say it: the top producers are not only in it for their clients. They are also in it for themselves. And good for them for doing it, as long as they do it responsibly and ethically.

Find your motivation, and you'll be clearer on money's role in supporting it.

Someone once said to me, "I don't think you are motivated by money." I quickly disagreed . . . but even more quickly realized that he was right. For me, the money is just the means to providing for my family. My family is my #1 motivator: braces, tuition, holidays, vacations, and birthday parties! Once I realized that, it was like I'd had horrible vision for years and finally got eyeglasses for the first time. It totally changed my perspective on staying motivated and in a good frame of mind.

As I have mentioned, in preparation for this book I conducted a number of interviews with advisors. I wanted as many opinions as I could get from advisors, but my only requirement was that they had to be producing gross revenues of over $1 million per year. I wanted to be sure that ideas and thoughts I would be writing about were vetted through real-life success—and not just my opinion.

I asked them many questions, as you might guess. The last question I asked them was "Why you? Why are you the one who reached production levels that only 1%–2% of the advisor community will reach?"

Every single advisor answered similarly. It was not meant as a leading question, but the answer was unanimous. It was always some version of this:

"Because I want it."

They *want* the success. And before you roll your eyes and say, "Clearly, I want it, too, or I wouldn't be suffering through this book!" Just pause.

Ask yourself if you really want it.

You know what has to be done and how, because the vetted strategies have been explained in these pages. Will you do it?

Do you want it enough to go the factory, day in and day out, and make the widgets? The answer from my interviewees was never "I do this work because I *love* prospecting." Likewise, their motivation was not that they excelled at the financial planning process, nor because the bank had really set them up for success. Those things may be true for some of them. But that's not *why* they do this work.

Top producers grind because they want it. They stop making excuses and go after what they want! They grit their teeth and get out of their comfort zone. They leave the house before their kids wake up when needed. They put the cell phone down and pick up the work phone.

Why? Because the long-term result is worth it to them. Because they want it. One very successful advisor said to me, "I got it made because I got it made."

Go make it!

ABOUT THE AUTHOR

 **Alex Spencer** has over 20 years' experience in the insurance and financial services industry. He has served as a financial advisor, sales manager, national sales manager, and wholesaler, working exclusively in the bank and credit union channel.

Having partnered with hundreds of financial advisors over his career, Alex has the in-depth knowledge of what the most successful advisors in banks and credit unions do to be successful. He takes special pride in helping others build their business and achieve success.

Alex resides in San Antonio, Texas with his wife, Annie, and their five children, Olivia, Sophia, Lulu, Croix, and Leo.

He holds a Bachelor of Arts degree from the University of Texas in Austin and the following licenses: Series 7, 24, 63, 65 and Texas Life & Health. He is a Chartered Retirement Planning Counselor (CRPC®) and Certified Social Security Claiming Strategist (CSSCS®).

ACKNOWLEDGMENTS

Thank you:

To my friends and mentors Gary Weuve and Don Connelly.

To the hundreds of advisors who invited me into their office to discuss their business, especially those who put extra work into helping me understand their business and to write this book: Jon Thompson, Justin Dams, Joe Barreca, Richard Abaunza, John Boles, Ross Kantor, Glenda Lossett, Randall Harris, Don Lutz, Jeff Hamm, Michael Packman, Juanita McCormick, Everett Franks, Angel Tavera, Rodney Horelka, Thomas McNeill, Melanie Weischwill, Caleb Staudt, John Eyster, and Jeff Heard.

To Austin LaVelle and Keith Pinkley for their patience, partnership and collaboration during the process.

And to those who took a chance on me and gave me an opportunity in this business, all of whom I have learned from: Terry Galindo, Ramiro Morales, Brett Giles, David Foster, Kelly Tramontano, and Rod Mims.

Made in the USA
Columbia, SC
22 April 2024